Culture and
Customs of
Colombia

Caribbean Sea

Panama

Pacific
Ocean

Santa
Marta
Ríohacha
Guajira

Barranquilla
Atlántico

Cartagena

Valledupar

Magdalena

César

Sincelejo

Montería

Sucre

Bolívar

Norte
de
Santander

Córdoba

Chocó

Cúcuta

Venezuela

Antioquia

Bucaramanga

Medellín

Santander

Arauca

Arauca

Quibdó

Boyacá

Casanare

Puerto
Carreño

1   2   3
Manizales
Pereira
Armenia

Tunja

Yopal

Vichada

Valle
del
Cauca

4
Ibagué

6
Bogotá

5

Villavicencio

Cali

Meta

Guainía

Cauca

Neiva

Popayán

San José del
Guaviare

Nariño

Huila

Guaviare

San Felipe

Pasto

Florencia

Mocoa

Mitú

Vaupés

Caquetá

Ecuador

Amazonas

Brazil

Colombia

⊕ National Capital
⊙ Department Capital

Central Provinces

1. Risaralda
2. Caldas
3. Cundinamarca
4. Quindío
5. Tolima
6. Distrito Especial

0   100   200 km
0   100 mi

Peru

Leticia

© 1999 maps.com

Culture and Customs of Colombia

Raymond Leslie Williams
and
Kevin G. Guerrieri

Culture and Customs of Latin America
and the Caribbean
Peter Standish, Series Editor

GREENWOOD PRESS
Westport, Connecticut • London

Library of Congress Cataloging-in-Publication Data

Williams, Raymond L.
    Culture and customs of Colombia / Raymond Leslie Williams, Kevin
    G. Guerrieri.
        p.   cm.—(Culture and customs of Latin America and the
    Caribbean   ISSN 1521–8856)
        Includes bibliographical references (p. –) and index.
        ISBN 0–313–30405–X (alk. paper)
        1. Colombia—Civilization—20th century.   2. Arts, Modern—20th
    century–Colombia.   3. Arts, Colombian.   4. Popular culture—
    Colombia.   5. Colombia—Social life and customs.   I. Guerrieri,
    Kevin G., 1970– .   II. Title.   III. Series.
    F2279.W55   1999
    986.106′35—dc21   98–51893

British Library Cataloguing in Publication Data is available.

Library of Congress Catalog Card Number: 98–51893
ISBN: 0–313–30405–X
ISSN: 1521–8856

First published in 1999

Greenwood Press, 88 Post Road West, Westport, CT 06881
An imprint of Greenwood Publishing Group, Inc.
www.greenwood.com

Printed in the United States of America

For Otto Morales Benítez

Contents

Illustrations   ix

Series Foreword   xi

Preface   xiii

Introduction   xv

Chronology   xvii

1   Context   1

2   Religion   15

3   Social Customs and Daily Life   25

4   The Media   43

5   The Performing Arts: Cinema, Theater, and Music   63

6   Literature   79

7   Gabriel García Márquez: The Writer and the Man   97

8   The Plastic Arts, Photography, and Architecture   117

Notes   131

Glossary   135

Bibliography   139

Index   143

Illustrations

Rural Antioquia	2
Traditional village, Antioquia	3
Traditional and modern in Bogotá	8
Village life in western valley	26
Traditional highland clothing	28
Carnaval in Barranquilla	30
Carnaval masks, Barranquilla	31
Daily life in downtown Cartagena	39
Writers Manuel Mejía Vallejo, Alonso Aristizábal, and Fanny Buitrago	81
Belisario Betancur, president of Colombia, 1982–1986	103
Mural by Alejandro Obregón in Barranquilla	119
Republican-style architecture in rural Antioquia	127
Residence from the 1920s in Barranquilla	128
Medellín	129

Series Foreword

"CULTURE" is a problematic word. In everyday language we tend to use it in at least two senses. On the one hand we speak of cultured people and places full of culture, uses that imply a knowledge or presence of certain forms of behavior or of artistic expression that are socially prestigious. In this sense large cities and prosperous people tend to be seen as the most cultured. On the other hand, there is an interpretation of "culture" that is broader and more anthropological; culture in this broader sense refers to whatever traditions, beliefs, customs, and creative activities characterize a given community—in short, it refers to what makes that community different from others. In this second sense, everyone has culture; indeed, it is impossible to be without culture.

The problems associated with the idea of culture have been exacerbated in recent years by two trends: less respectful use of language and a greater blurring of cultural differences. Nowadays, "culture" often means little more than behavior, attitude, or atmosphere. We hear about the culture of the boardroom, of the football team, of the marketplace; there are books with titles like *The Culture of War* by Richard Gabriel (Greenwood, 1990) or *The Culture of Narcissism* by Christopher Lasch (1979). In fact, as Christopher Clausen points out in a recent article published in the *American Scholar* (Summer 1996), we have gotten ourselves into trouble by using the term so sloppily.

People who study culture generally assume that culture (in the anthropological sense) is learned, not genetically determined. Another general assumption made in these days of multiculturalism has been that cultural differences should be respected rather than put under pressure to change. But these assumptions, too, have sometimes proved to be problematic. For instance, multiculturalism is a fine ideal, but in practice it is not always easy to reconcile with the beliefs of the very people who advocate it: for example, is female circumcision an issue of human rights or just a different cultural practice?

The blurring of cultural differences is a process that began with the steamship, increased with radio, and is now racing ahead with the Internet. We are becoming globally homogenized. Since the English-speaking world (and the United States in particular) is the dominant force behind this process of homogenization, it behooves us to make efforts to understand the sensibilities of members of other cultures.

This series of books, a contribution toward that greater understanding, deals with the neighbors of the United States, with people who have just as much right to call themselves Americans. What are the historical, institutional, religious, and artistic features that make up the modern culture of such peoples as the Haitians, the Chileans, the Jamaicans, and the Guatemalans? How are their habits and assumptions different from our own? What can we learn from them? As we familiarize ourselves with the ways of other countries, we come to see our own from a new perspective.

Each volume in the series focuses on a single country. With slight variations to accommodate national differences, each begins by outlining the historical, political, ethnic, geographical, and linguistic context, as well as the religious and social customs, and then proceeds to a discussion of a variety of artistic activities, including the press, the media, the cinema, music, literature, and the visual and performing arts. The authors are all intimately acquainted with the countries concerned: some were born or brought up in them, and each has a professional commitment to enhancing the understanding of the culture in question.

We are inclined to suppose that our ways of thinking and behaving are normal. And so they are . . . for us. We all need to realize that ours is only one culture among many, and that it is hard to establish by any rational criteria that ours as a whole is any better (or worse) than any other. As individual members of our immediate community, we know that we must learn to respect our differences from one another. Respect for differences between cultures is no less vital. This is particularly true of the United States, a nation of immigrants, but one that sometimes seems to be bent on destroying variety at home, and, worse still, on having others follow suit. By learning about other people's cultures, we come to understand and respect them; we earn their respect for us, and, not least, we see ourselves in a new light.

Peter Standish
East Carolina University

Preface

This project is the result of some twenty-three years of experience in Colombia, beginning in 1975 when I lived there for a year and began initial research on the Colombian novel. Since then, I have returned annually for periods ranging from a few days to a few months. Since the late 1980s, I have been taking notes and accumulating materials for a book such as this—a general introduction to the culture and customs of Colombia directed to the nonspecialist reader. Thanks to three different grants, I have been able to enjoy extended stays in Colombia for formal research and learning about daily life there from my own experience.

The generosity and assistance of numerous Colombians over the past two decades have made it possible for me to gain special access to materials and insights that would have been difficult or impossible to gain without their goodwill. A list of all these individuals would be impractical to publish and inevitably would fail to include everyone deserving of mention. Nevertheless, I will mention a limited number of Colombians whose exceptional generosity and goodwill since 1975 have been most appreciated: Gustavo Alvarez Gardeazábal, Belisario Betancur, Darío Jaramillo Agudelo, Alfonso López Michelsen, Otto Morales Benítez, Gloria Inés de Palomino, and the now-deceased Germán Vargas.

In different stages of this book, research assistants and others have been extremely supportive in helping me locate specific materials needed for the eight chapters. In the early stages of this project, undergraduate research assistants Lindsay Anderson, John Dorsey, Angela Espinosa, and Erin Minks did exemplary work, as did graduate assistant Ana Mercedes Patiño. In the latter stages,

Carlos Peñaranda and Martha Ponce de León provided generous support and assistance in Bogotá. My colleagues, William Megenney and Marina Pianca, also offered useful materials that facilitated my research.

In the final stages, Kevin Guerrieri assumed such an essential role that I offered him recognition as coauthor. At that point, he wrote the entire first draft of chapter 4 and assisted in the editing of the entire volume. He also accepted a major role in working with the editors of this series to take the book from the manuscript to its final form. Nevertheless, the content of this book is my responsibility, as are any errors of fact or judgment that might be found.

Raymond Leslie Williams

Introduction

Located on the northern part of the South American continent, Colombia has coasts on both the Pacific and Atlantic sides of Panama. The nation has been internationally recognized as one of the world's major coffee producers and as the homeland of world-class writers, such as Gabriel García Márquez, painters, and sculptors, as well as popular music composers. However, their achievements have been overshadowed in the latter part of the century by Colombia's role in the international trafficking of illegal drugs.

Today, Colombia is one of the most violent nations in the world. A variety of armed guerrilla groups have been active in Colombia since the 1960s, and since the 1980s, guerrilla groups armed by drug traffickers have created an increasingly serious problem of national security and assassinations. The homicide rate in Colombia, in fact, was the highest in the Western Hemisphere during the 1990s. The guerrilla groups tend to operate in isolated rural areas, where they enter into conflict with the military; drug traffickers and petty criminals operate in the urban spaces of Bogotá, Medellín, and Cali, and sometimes in smaller cities.

Despite these problems and the threats to both the citizenry and national security in general, Colombia has managed to maintain one of the longest-standing democratic political systems in Latin America. No other Latin American nation has witnessed the survival of its two traditional parties from the nineteenth century. Relations between the respective governments of Colombia and the United States have been generally amicable, with the most notable tensions between the two nations occurring in the early part of the century over the issue of Panama, and the latter part of the century over the issue of drug trafficking.

Most middle-class Colombians, who have nothing to do with illegal drugs or stereotypes of Juan Valdés (the television image of the coffee picker), have had to suffer from a grossly exaggerated negative image. Colombia is also a nation with special features of international impact, which are far less known. It was a pioneer in promoting air transportation, constructing one of the earliest national airline systems in the West in the 1920s. Colombia is rich in agricultural production, and its Valle del Cauca is one of only three regions in the world that can produce sugar year-round. In recent decades, Colombia has also been a major exporter of flowers to the United States and has become an exporter of petroleum.

Intense conflicts and ongoing political crises have affected all sectors of social and economic life but paradoxically, several spheres of Colombian culture have flourished, particularly since the 1960s. Colombia is a special case with respect to its writers and painters. Gabriel García Márquez has won international acclaim for his novels associated with the setting of the mythical Macondo and was awarded the Nobel Prize for Literature in 1982. His fiction, which always questioned traditional values and society in Colombia and Latin America, culminated in the masterpiece *Cien años de soledad* (*One Hundred Years of Solitude*, 1967). Three contemporary painters of the same generation have become recognized as world-class artists since the 1950s: Alejandro Obregón, Fernando Botero, and Enrique Grau. Obregón's pioneer work portrays much of the Caribbean physical world that García Márquez recreates in his fiction set in Macondo (see chapter 7). Botero's irreverent and satirical painting and sculpture always carries the trademark of oversized human figures. His paintings satire a variety of sectors of the Colombian oligarchy, from the politicians and the socialites to the church hierarchy. Grau is equally accomplished as a master technician and modernizing force in Colombian painting as Obregón and Botero (see chapter 8).

Colombia has been a leader in Latin America in the production of certain kinds of popular music for both listening and dancing. The *cumbia*, one of Latin America's most popular dance rhythms in recent decades, has its origins from the Caribbean (see chapter 5). Colombian Carlos Vives has become an internationally recognized singer of Caribbean tunes; since the 1980s, the *vallenato* has become as popular throughout the Hispanic world as the *cumbia* (see chapter 5).

For those interested in a comparative understanding of Latin American nations, Colombia is a special and interesting case study for at least three reasons: its extreme regionalism, its deeply rooted traditionalism, and the marked presence of the Catholic Church in daily and institutional life. These three factors appear and reappear in the facets of Colombian culture and customs reviewed and analyzed in the chapters that follow.

Chronology

1525   The first Spanish colonial city, Santa Marta, is founded in Colombia by Rodrigo de Bastidas.

1535   Popayán, a city in the greater Cauca, is founded.

1536   The Valle del Cauca's largest city, Cali, is founded.

1580   *Los Alarcos* is the first Spanish play to be presented in Colombia.

1616   Greater Antioquia's major city, Medellín, is founded.

1622   The Jesuits found the Pontificia Universidad Javeriana.

1629   Fernando Fernández de Valenzuela writes the play *Laura crítica*.

1638   *El carnero*, a major work of narrative prose, is completed.

1741   The Jesuits bring the first printing press to Colombia.

1767   The Jesuits are officially expelled from Colombia.

1774   The Jesuits found the University of San José in Popayán.

1791   The first true newspaper of Colombia is printed: the *Papel Periódico de la Ciudad de Santa Fe de Bogotá*.

1793   The Coliseo Ramírez, a major theater building, is constructed.

1810   Colombia proclaims independence from Spain.

1831   After the separation of Venezuela and Ecuador, the República de Nueva Granada is founded.

1839 News about European photographic technology first appears in the Colombian press.

1844 Colombia's first novel, Juan José Nieto's *Ingermina*, is published.

1851 Slavery is abolished in Colombia.

1855 *El Tiempo* newspaper is founded under the direction of José María Samper.

1858 Eugenio Díaz's novel *Manuela* first appears, published in *El Mosaico*.

1863 One of the most liberal constitutions in Latin America (at that time) is written but is overthrown within a year. This constitution ratifies the idea of the nation as a collection of sovereign states.

1867 Jorge Isaacs's novel *María* is published.

1886 The writing of a new constitution marks the end of a quarter century of Liberal Party leadership and the beginning of the Regeneration.

1887 A concordat is passed institutionalizing the Catholic Church's long-standing role in Colombia. Fidel Cano founds the newspaper *El Espectador*.

1891 Photographer Meltón Rodríguez's work first appears.

1892 The Teatro Colón is opened, replacing the Coliseo Ramírez.

1896 José María Vergara y Vergara produces the play *El espíritu del siglo*. Tomás Carrasquilla's first major novel, *Frutos de mi tierra*, is published.

1899 The War of a Thousand Days breaks out between the liberals and the conservatives.

1903 Panama, previously a department of Colombia, gains its sovereignty.

1905 Lorenzo Marroquín writes the play *Lo irremediable*.

1908 The Di Domenico family from Italy begins showing films in Bogotá and Medellín.

1917 The cultural magazine *Voces* is first published.

1918 Conservative Marco Fidel Suárez, one of the last *presidentes gramáticos*, is elected president.

1919 Daniel Lemaitre creates the first *bolero* in Colombia.

1924 José Eustacio Rivera's *La vorágine* is published.

1927 The Cine Colombia is founded. José Féliz Fuenmayor's novel *Cosme* is published.

1928 Gabriel García Márquez is born in Aracataca.

1929 Elías Pellet Buitrago premieres Colombia's first radio broadcast.

1930 Liberal Enrique Olaya Herrera is elected president.

1934 Newly elected president Alfonso López Pumarejo initiates La Revolución en Marcha, a program of reformist liberalism.

1935 Internationally known singer Carlos Gardel dies in plane crash, an event leading to the birth of Colombian radio journalism.

1936 The School of Architecture is founded in the Universidad Nacional, an important factor in the ongoing modernization of urban spaces in Colombia.

1937 The National Federation of Coffee Growers is created to protect smaller growers.

1941 The Instituto Etnológico Nacional is founded in an attempt to give voice to the indigenous population.

1944 The Roman Catholic Church in Europe establishes the Catholic Social Action program. President Alfonso López Pumarejo is taken prisoner by Colonel Heriberto Gil during a military coup.

1946 The Jesuits found the urban trade union Unión de Trabajadores de Colombia (UTC).

1947 Le Corbusier, whose influence is later to be seen in Colombian architecture, arrives in the country.

1948 La Violencia is ignited on April 9 when the populist candidate Jorge Eliécer Gaitán, representing the Liberal Party, is assassinated in Bogotá. This incident, including the subsequent popular uprising, is known as the *Bogotazo*. CARACOL, one of the first major radio networks, is founded.

1949 The priest José Joaquín Salcedo initiates "Radio Sutatenza," a program based on teaching literacy to rural workers.

1950 The cultural radio station HJCK is founded.

1953 Octavio Marulanda founds the theater group Artistas del Pueblo.

1954 The inauguration of television in Colombia takes place.

1955 Gabriel García Márquez's novel *La hojarasca* is published. The magazine *Mito* is first published.

1958 Peace accords between the liberals and the conservatives create a systematic sharing of power between the two parties, thus marking the unofficially recognized end of La Violencia.

1961 The Agrarian Reform Law is passed.

1962 Gabriel García Márquez's *Los funerales de la mamá grande*, Alvaro Cepeda Samudio's *La casa grande*, and Héctor Rojas Herazo's *Respirando el verano* are published.

1963 *Inravisión*, the National Institute of Radio and Television, is founded. Colombia's first *telenovela*, "In the Name of Love," is broadcast.

1964 Manuel Mejía Vallejo's novel *El día señalado* is published.

1965 Father Camilo Torres announces the formation of a new political coalition, the *Frente Unido*. Torres is killed in combat against government soldiers the following year.

1966 The forty-floor Avianca building is completed, making it the tallest structure in Bogotá.

1967 Gabriel García Márquez's *Cien años de soledad* is published. *Pasado al meridiano* and *Camilo Torres*, two significant films, mark a turning point in the film industry.

1968 The CELAM conference in Medellín calls for reforms of basic church institutions in Colombia and Latin America. The Pope visits Colombia.

1970 The national election causes political crisis. The urban guerrilla movement M-19 is founded.

1972 Jorge Silva and Marta Rodríguez's film *Chircales* is produced.

1973 A new concordat is signed by President Misael Pastrana and church officials, which modifies the Catholic Church's status as the official state religion.

1975 Gabriel García Márquez's novel *El otoño del patriarca* is published.

1982 Gabriel García Márquez is awarded the Nobel Prize.

1984 Francisco Norden's film *Cóndores no entierran todos los días* is produced.

1985 Inravisión is restructured, and regional television channels are inaugurated shortly thereafter (1985–1992).

1986 Newly elected Virgilio Barco undertakes an active government campaign against the drug cartels. Guillermo Cano, editor of *El Espectador*, is slain in an ambush by drug traffickers.

1989   Television and radio journalist Jorge Enrique Pulido is assassinated by drug traffickers.

1996   *Noticia de un secuestro*, by Gabriel García Márquez, is published. Fabio Salgado Mejía, known as "Estéfano," is awarded a Grammy for his *bolero* "Mi tierra."

1998   Víctor Gaviria's film *La vendedora de rosas* is recognized at the Cannes Film Festival.

1

Context

GEOGRAPHY

Colombia is Latin America's fifth largest nation, with 440,000 square miles. Its three Andean ranges (*cordilleras*) are separated by two major rivers—the Magdalena, which flows into the Caribbean, and the Cauca, which flows into the Pacific. The population centers are located in the plateaus and basins among these ranges and in the valleys of the two rivers. The northern (Caribbean) lowlands consist of open land used for agriculture and raising cattle. The western (Pacific) lowlands are sparsely populated and consist of large portions of forests, jungle, and swamps. A vast interior plain spreads east of the Andes, with open land in the north and jungle to the south.

Colombia's topographic conformation has been a key factor in the development of the nation's regionalism. The mountain ranges, composed of three *cordilleras*, have posed enormous obstacles to any kind of national unity. Interregional transportation, economic activity, communication, and cultural activity have always been challenging and frequently nonexistent. Rather than looking to a neighboring region or the capital, the Colombian who has turned outward has traditionally been more likely to look abroad. Notable examples of this phenomenon are two such markedly different cases as the nineteenth-century tobacco industry and the literary career of the twentieth century's Gabriel García Márquez. For the tobacco merchant of Ambalema and the novelist from Aracataca, the roots are local, and the extralocal contact is international, not interregional. Colombia's acute regionalism developed in this fashion.

Rural Antioquia

REGIONALISM

Throughout its history, Colombia has been one of the most markedly regionalist nations in Latin America. In the nineteenth century, Colombia was a loose coalition of four semiautonomous regions: the interior highland, greater Antioquia, the Caribbean coastal region, and greater Cauca. The interior highland includes the area of Bogotá and the present-day departments of Cundinamarca, Boyacá, Santander, Norte de Santander, Tolima, and Huila.[1] Characteristics of interior highland culture are a dominant Spanish heritage, a sophisticated literary culture, and a sparse presence of oral culture in literature. The region's indigenous population was decimated during the conquest and colonial period, and Colombia's Afro-American population has never been large in Bogotá.

The region of greater Antioquia includes present-day departments of Antioquia, Caldas, Risaralda, and Quindío. The culture of this region has been willfully independent of the remainder of Colombia and quite often in direct opposition to it. An indigenous population of approximately 600,000 inhabited Antioquia at the time of the conquest, but conflicts and disease swiftly reduced their numbers. The inhabitants of Antioquia during the colonial period

Traditional village, Antioquia

lacked the capital necessary to bring African slaves from Cartagena. Consequently, gold seekers from Antioquia went searching as independent prospectors: many of the Spaniards, as well as later generations of *criollos* (Caucasians of Spanish bloodlines born in Colombia), were thus forced into productive labor on their own account. This situation gave an early impetus to Antioquia's egalitarian work ethic. The tradition of independence and egalitarianism, however, did not contribute to Antioquia's cultural development during the colonial period. On the contrary, most observers were struck by the general backwardness, illiteracy, and poverty of the province until the end of the colonial period.

Greater Antioquia's major city, Medellín, founded in 1616, was little more than a village during the first half of the nineteenth century. The image and memory of Medellín-the-village and the traditional life around it became a source of much nostalgic fiction in Antioquia (see chapter 6). Key factors in Medellín's transformation from village to city were the markedly increased cof-

fee production from the 1880s forward, and the foundation of the textile industry by the end of the century. Nascent industrialization was further evident
in the fact that ten factories were in place by 1900. A direct relationship operated between increased coffee production and industrialization: Coffee created
the market and the capital for the subsequent industrialization.

The Caribbean coastal region includes the departments of Magdalena,
Bolívar, César, Sucre, Córdoba, and Guajira. While highland culture has a predominantly Spanish heritage, with its venerable Hispanic literary tradition
representing an elitist literary culture, coastal culture is triethnic in heritage
and represents a popular and oral culture. The highland has been conservative,
closed, and unreceptive to change. The Caribbean coast, on the other hand,
with its port cities, has been more receptive to outside influences and innovation in numerous areas, from architecture to literature. Coastal oral culture has
coexisted with writing culture, the former located primarily in the small towns
and rural areas on the coast, and the latter in the cities. The vast differences between the culture of a town such as Aracataca (of García Márquez, see chapter
7) and a city such as Barranquilla in the 1920s, for example, or between Cartagena and Chimá in the 1880s, are evidence of the phenomenon that Fals Borda
has described as the uneven development of the coastal region.[2]

The African presence on the Caribbean coast relates directly to the slave re-
bellions during the colonial period that led to the founding of villages (*palenques*) of black rebels, some of which have survived for centuries, such as
Palenque de San Basilio, a village located between Cartagena and Mompox.
Palenque de San Basilio, in fact, can be seen as the opposite pole to Cartagena's
Spanish and lettered aristocracy: It has consisted entirely of runaway African
slaves, virtually isolated for more than three centuries from the writing culture
of the Caribbean coastal cities. Even as late as 1924, the year José Eustacio Rivera's *La vorágine* (*The Vortex*) was a bestseller in the remainder of Colombia,
contact between Palenque de San Basilio and the rest of the nation was tenu-
ous.[3] This isolated Afro-Colombian culture has developed its own language,
palenquero, the only Spanish-based creole language in the Western Hemisphere.[4] The case of Palenque de San Basilio is perhaps the most extreme example, but certainly not the only one that could be cited that points to the
heterogeneity and uneven development of the oral-based triethnic culture of
the Caribbean coast.[5]

Unlike the comparatively isolated and conventional Bogotá, twentieth-
century Barranquilla has been more progressive and receptive to foreign influences, perhaps because it is a port city. North American Karl C. Parrish contributed to the modern architectural layout of the El Prado neighborhood, still
present in Barranquilla.

Greater Cauca consists of the present-day departments of Valle del Cauca, Cauca, Nariño, Putumayo, and Chocó. This region, which is centered in the Valle del Cauca but includes Popayán (founded in 1535) to the south and Chocó to the north, has developed a tradition of cultural heterogeneity. Since the colonial period, Popayán has been a bastion of elitist writing culture. The Jesuits founded the University of San José in Popayán in 1774. The Valle del Cauca, with Cali (founded in 1536) as its largest city, has felt the influence of an opulent aristocracy and also of the populist forces represented by the minority African Colombian population and the Antioquian pioneers who settled its northern and eastern parts in the nineteenth and twentieth centuries. The Chocó (northern) area of this region, has been geographically and culturally isolated and sparsely populated.

The egalitarian traditions of greater Antioquia can be contrasted with a vastly different situation in greater Cauca. Until well into the twentieth century, this region's society had a markedly stratified class structure with a small lettered elite and generally illiterate masses. This generalization echoes the description of the interior highland region. Indeed, one of the centers of the colonial lettered power structure was Popayán, a city that compares favorably to its counterparts in Tunja and Bogotá in both its colonial architectural splendor and its venerable literary traditions. Popayán also represented a similarly conservative Hispanic model. Despite these similarities, one must avoid the facile and superficial conclusion that greater Cauca is a western Colombian replica of the interior highland model. The historical and cultural denominators are far too complex in greater Cauca to allow for such a simplification. The region's complexity can be seen in Cali, a city with a small elite in the nineteenth century which became a modern, industrialized city in the twentieth century, the strongly Afro-Colombian region of Chocó, and a triethnic racial makeup whose indigenous presence is the most pronounced of the four regions during the last two centuries.

The indigenous and black African populations of greater Cauca have lived with the Hispanic inhabitants since the sixteenth century, suffering different degrees of exploitation or extermination, depending on the period and the specific area of the region. By 1511, the Spaniards knew of the gold in the Chocó region, and African slaves were the primary source of labor in the mines. The Indian population that was present throughout most parts of greater Cauca was rapidly decimated; nevertheless, the department of Cauca has the largest Indian population of any department of Colombia, with slightly more than 100,000 of the approximate half-million Native American inhabitants in the nation.

To nineteenth-century visionaries, whose hopes of regional progress were constantly being swept away by political chaos and economic instability, today's greater Cauca would appear to be a promise fulfilled. The vibrant and progressive city of Cali is for many—particularly civic-minded *caleños*—a veritable monument to the possibilities of modern urban development in Latin America. The region's vast expanses of abundant land, fertile for agriculture and rich in minerals, have afforded the area economic prosperity. The Valle del Cauca is one of only three regions in the world that can produce sugar year-round. Wealthy families of the Valle del Cauca's large landowning oligarchy, with names such as Caicedo, Garcés, and Lourido (some of which are still the mainstays of the region's elite), were financially prosperous and politically powerful during the seventeenth and eighteenth centuries.

In the nineteenth century, greater Cauca's heterogeneity was stimulated by a series of factors which radically changed the makeup of the region's society and culture. A key turning point was the abolition of slavery in Colombia in 1851, a severe blow to the interests of the large landowning elite. The region suffered economic stagnation during much of the second half of the nineteenth century. The 1890s saw an economic recovery; nevertheless, as on the Caribbean coast, it was a case of uneven development. For example, one observer has spoken of the curious juxtaposition of the modern and the premodern; in a region with several elite writers, the majority of the populace in the 1880s was illiterate. During the 1920s, Cali, like Colombia's other major cities, underwent a process of modernization. The train line connecting Cali to the port city of Buenaventura, completed in 1915, was an important predecessor to this transformation. Modern technology for sugar refining was introduced to the Valle del Cauca in the 1920s. The clearest indicator of Cali's industrialization was the presence of seventy-seven factories in the 1930s, compared to only one at the turn of the century.

Many Latin American countries have regional differences and geographies not conducive to cultural unity, but Colombia's barriers to national integrity have been exceptionally deep-rooted and prohibitive. For example, geographic and political factors have combined to give Colombia a railroad system markedly inferior to those of Mexico, Argentina, or Brazil since the turn of the century: A measure of Colombia's slowness to adopt the railways is shown in the period 1880–1910, during which Colombia built an additional 21 percent of its total, Mexico added 79 percent of its railways, Argentina added 59 percent, and Brazil added 49 percent.[6] Ground transportation has always been extremely difficult in Colombia; the Magdalena River has been the only natural source of interregional connection. As late as the 1920s, a reporter from the United States wrote that "the departments of Antioquia and Cundinamarca are the only ones in Colombia where wagon roads of any length extending outside the towns are found."[7] A concentrated, systematic effort to build the nation's highway system was carried out only from the 1930s forward, with the rise of the modern state.

Perhaps the most conclusive example of the impact of Colombian regionalism and of its historical base in the nineteenth century is the regionalist legacy of Rafael Núñez. Núñez wrote that Colombia "is not a single nationality, but a group of nationalities, each one needing its own special, independent, and exclusive government."[8] The decline of liberalism and the emergence of Núñez and the conservatives in the 1880s demonstrate that regionalist tensions were a deep-rooted, permanent feature of nineteenth-century Colombia and not a temporary result of the uneven effect of changes in the international market affecting Colombian exports. The elections of 1875, for example, were fought along regional lines. Though hardly unique in its composition of sections along geographic and economic lines, Colombia "differs from other countries of similar size in the deep imprint its regionalist sentiment has left on the pattern of regional development."[9]

Seen historically, the development of Colombia's regionalism falls into three basic periods: the colonial stage, from the sixteenth century to the 1830s; the republic's regional division, from the 1830s to the 1950s; and the postregional period of the modern state. During the first stage, the region of New Granada (as it was called by Spain during the colonial period), in geographic isolation, began to develop regional identities based in part on variations in the ethnic mix. During this time, the indigenous population was decimated. Relatively small numbers of the indigenous groups remained intact in isolated areas, particularly in the areas of greater Cauca and Guajira; a mestizo culture developed in greater Antioquia, while Antioquia saw the end of any significant indigenous heritage. Entrepeneurs brought African slaves to New Granada, primarily into the lowland regions, but also into the present-day area of Antioquia. The interior highland, meanwhile, maintained a strong Hispanic heritage, and a triethnic racial and cultural situation emerged in the other regions. Political, economic, and cultural power of the colonial period was centered in the old colonial cities: Bogotá, Popayán, Cartagena, and, to a lesser extent, Tunja, Santa Fe de Antioquia, Cali, and Mompos. Communication among these colonial cities and their surrounding regions, even by standards of the times, remained slow and often treacherous.

In the 1850s, certain political, economic, and cultural factors began to change, but with differing levels of intensity and impact in the various regions. In the political arena, the two traditional parties had developed a sense of identity by mid-century. The abolition of slavery in 1851 affected the ethnic com-

Traditional and modern in Bogotá

position of some regions; for example, Afro-American former slaves in Antioquia tended to move to the Caribbean coastal region. The Constitution of 1863 ratified the idea of a nation as a collection of sovereign states; the period of its being in effect, 1864 to 1886, saw the maximum institutionalized political expression of regional autonomy.

Although the political consolidation that took place in 1886 signaled a return to what would become nearly a half century of conservative rule, national unity was still more a political ideal than an economic, social, or cultural unity. Poor interregional transportation meant that much economic development remained local. And cultural activity was typically regional: at the turn of the century the traditional and realist *escuela antioqueña* (Antioquian school) was opposed to the *modernista* intellectuals of Bogotá. The *costumbrista* writers celebrated regional values.

Colombia's transition from isolated regions to a more unified nation took place between the 1930s and 1950s. The governments of the Liberal Republic invested heavily in the railway and highway systems; the advent of air transportation in the 1920s opened new possibilities. An unprecedented immigration from the rural areas to the cities—above all, Bogotá—began in the 1930s. Bogotá was opening to the outside world as it never had before.

The transition from a strictly regionalist to a more national and even international outlook shaped cultural activities. Artists and architects began association with what was called the "international" style (see chapter 8). While much of Antioquian Tomás Carrasquilla's later fiction (published in the 1920s and 1930s) lamented the loss of traditional values of Antioquia in favor of the growing modernity, other writers, such as José Félix Fuenmayor in Barranquilla and José Antonio Osorio Lizarazo in Bogotá, novelized themes related to the new, urban settings (see chapter 6). If Cartagena had symbolized regional power during the colonial period, the rise of Barranquilla in the twentieth century was representative of a new, modern order on the Caribbean coast. Cultural life in general began to change radically after the 1930s. One example is the history of newspaper production in small towns. Before the 1930s, small towns often produced several local newspapers; after the 1930s, when the roads from Bogotá were completed, many of these regional newspapers disappeared in favor of the newly available national newspaper, *El Tiempo* (for further discussion of the press, see chapter 4).

The third stage of Colombia's regional development is the postregional period from the 1950s to the present. By the 1950s, modernization, industrialization, and immigration to the cities had reshaped many of the previous regional boundaries. La Violencia, an undeclared civil war of that time, was a phenomenon that affected the national psyche, not simply a regional conflict. The establishment of national radio networks in the 1940s and national television channels in the 1950s was extremely important to Colombia's postregional development. The number of national flights on Avianca increased dramatically in the post–World War II period. The nation had been at war for more than a century over regional versus central political power. The formation of the National Front in 1958 contributed significantly to national rather than regional unity and identity in the political sphere. Many Colombians remain staunchly regionalist in their mind-set and political convictions. Nevertheless, in the past five decades Colombia has became a nation in an area of Latin America that for several centuries was a loose collection of semiautonomous political states with clearly defined cultural differences.

HISTORY

The Spaniards began their conquest of the region that they called New Granada (Colombia) in 1531, and had taken control of the indigenous population in most regions by 1539. They entered from present-day Quito, Ecuador, to explore and conquer the upper Cauca Valley, founding Cali in 1536. Gonzalo Jiménez de Quesada conquered Bacatá and founded a new city near the current

Bogotá in 1538. The colonial administration of New Granada was the same as the rest of the colonies. New Granada was generally less profitable than New Spain (Mexico) or Peru.

Simón Bolívar is still revered as the liberator of Colombia; after three centuries of colonial rule from Madrid, Bolívar spearheaded the military victory against the Spanish army, the decisive battle taking place in Boyacá in 1819. The nineteenth century in Colombia was characterized by intense conflicts between partisans of the Liberal and Conservative parties. The Conservative Party has traditionally been a supporter of a powerful Catholic Church and has tended to be supported by the landed aristocracy. The Liberal Party has been more associated with middle sectors of Colombian society (often including the merchant class), although neither of these generalizations holds true entirely, for some members of the conservative oligarchy were merchants and some members of the Liberal Party have been landowners.

The period from 1810 to 1862 comprised the formative years for the new nation, which proclaimed independence in 1810, and was characterized by conflict and crisis. Within two years, the first of innumerable civil wars between centralists and federalists occurred, a point of contention in almost all the nineteenth-century civil wars.

Conflicts between conservatives and liberals—played out primarily as tension between centralist versus republican forces—culminated in six civil wars during the nineteenth century. These wars frequently led to revised constitutions, the most notable of which was the Constitution of 1863. The most liberal constitution at the time in Latin America, this document provided for the separation of church and state, universal suffrage, and the autonomy of the provinces. This constitution was overthrown within a year, and centrifugal forces grew in the following decades, leading to the consolidation of conservative forces by 1903, and a series of conservative presidents until 1930.

The conservative reaction in the late nineteenth century was dominated by a figure of a very different stamp, former liberal Rafael Núñez. Among the novelists, José Manuel Marroquín, poet, linguist, president of Colombia, and, above all, conservative Hispanic highland gentleman-scholar, best embodies the spirit of the Regeneration. A seminal figure of the Regeneration, conservative politician and intellectual Miguel Antonio Caro was one of the writers of the new Constitution of 1886. In use for more than a century, this constitution marked the end of a quarter century of Liberal Party leadership. President Rafael Núñez's 1886 administration signaled the beginning of conservative power, adherence to a more Hispanic tradition, the principle of political centralization and administrative decentralization. The new constitution also reestablished strong relations between the Catholic Church and state. Under the

Regeneration, Marroquín and Miguel Caro, in addition to intellectuals such as Rufino José Caro, had the support from the power structure to undertake the creation of a Hellenic/Catholic Arcadia, previously yearned for by the writers José Eusebio Caro and Sergio Arboleda.

The conservative dominance of Bogotá, the Athens of South America (as it was called at the end of the nineteenth century), continued in the early twentieth century, perhaps best exemplified by one of the last major *presidentes gramáticos*, educator, linguist, diplomat, and essayist Marco Fidel Suárez, president from 1918 to 1921. But the Regeneration's ideological project did not go unchallenged; liberal strength gradually reasserted itself.

During the Regeneration, Colombia lost Panama (previously a "department" or state of Colombia), resulting in Panama's sovereignty in 1903. Colombians have pointed to the role of the United States government in supporting the independence movement, which created considerable friction between the two countries in the early part of the century.

The economic crisis ushered in by the depression in the late 1920s discredited the conservatives and resulted in the election of the liberal Enrique Olaya Herrera (1930–1934). Now the main agenda of the government, under Liberal Party rule, was social and economic reforms favoring workers. The 1930s and 1940s saw rapid and self-conscious modernization and industrialization under a series of liberal governments. The liberal project—the progressive modern state—began under Olaya Herrera, a mildly reformist president who governed a coalition of liberals and conservatives known as the National Concentration. He stimulated public housing, welfare and education programs, attempted land distribution, and fostered oil exploration. Alfonso López Pumarejo (1934–1938) undertook the most radical reforms of the Liberal Republic, with a program known as *La Revolución en Marcha*. Such measures as his land reform law of 1936 (Ley 200) attempted to eradicate the final vestiges of colonial economic and political structures and to accelerate the pace of modernization. This reformist liberalism of the 1930s and 1940s differed fundamentally from the romantic and philosophical liberalism of the nineteenth century. It represented a radical ideological change, giving voice to heretofore unheard liberal and revolutionary discourse. For example, the founding of the Instituto Etnológico Nacional in 1941 was an attempt to give voice to the largely ignored indigenous population.

Despite its violent first century, Colombia is the only Latin American nation in which the traditional political parties have survived from their nineteenth-century foundation to the present, and Colombia has been one of Latin America's most stable democracies in the twentieth century. Party rivalries produced outbreaks of violence in the 1930s and 1940s, culminating in an undeclared civil war identified as La Violencia during the 1950s, which resulted in approximately 300,000 deaths. This war was ignited on April 9, 1948, when the populist candidate representing the Liberal Party, Jorge Eliécer Gaitán, was assassinated in Bogotá. La Violencia is commonly dated from 1946 to 1958, however its roots have been traced to conflicts in the 1930s, and some social scientists believe the phenomenon still had not subsided in the 1980s. Although figures vary and are difficult to prove, it is generally agreed that 200,000 to 300,000 persons died during this sustained civil war.

Most of the conflicts between the two traditional parties were resolved with the peace accords of 1958, creating a systematic sharing of power between the liberals and conservatives, called the National Front. Since the 1960s, a variety of leftist guerrilla groups have been active in Colombia, some of which have been integrated into the institutional political system in recent years. (This is the case of the M-19, which was founded as an urban guerrilla movement in 1970.) The phenomenal rise of drug trafficking since the late 1970s has further destabilized political and social life in Colombia, particularly since the active government campaign of President Virgilio Barco (1986–1990) against the drug cartels.

ECONOMY

The wealth of the traditional aristocracy in Colombia has been based primarily on agriculture. Besides coffee, Colombia is also one of the main exporters of flowers to the United States. Colombia has abundant natural resources, such as metals and minerals, and is the world's major exporter of emeralds. It also produces petroleum for domestic consumption and some export.

In the 1970s, industry surpassed agriculture as the major contributor to the gross domestic product. Colombian industries, which often are family operated, include textiles, paper, chemicals, and basic metals. The manufacturing centers have been Bogotá, Medellín, and Cali. In the 1970s and 1980s, Bogotá accounted for approximately one quarter of total industrial production and one quarter of industrial employment. Medellín became a center of industry primarily because of inexpensive power available from the hydroelectric resources of surrounding areas. Cali accounts for approximately 20 percent of industrial production. Special government incentives have promoted some industry in Cartagena, Barranquilla, Manizales, and Barrancabermeja.

Coffee is the most important crop in Colombia and its major export. It is grown in the area Colombians call the "golden triangle" between Bogotá, Medellín, and Cali, which has Manizales as its geographic center. The National Federation of Coffee Growers was created in 1937 as an organization to protect the smaller grower at the national level. By the 1970s, it had become a pivotal agency in defining the country's coffee growing and selling policy, and was given semiofficial status.

After coffee, the next most important crops in Colombia are sugarcane, cotton, and rice. Most of the white sugar is grown on large estates in the Cauca Valley and along the Atlantic coast, and brown sugar, known as *panela*, is grown by small landholders and used mostly by rural inhabitants. (Urban Colombians tend to use white sugar.) Tightly controlled domestic prices for sugar have resulted in a tendency to smuggle sugar illegally out of the country to receive much higher prices. Cotton farms range from very small to large plantations, and are located primarily on the Caribbean coast. Much of the rice is cultivated in the department of Tolima. Colombians also raise bananas for both domestic use and export. Other crops—far less important for the national economy—are wheat, barley, oilseeds, tobacco, potatoes, cacao, and many kinds of cassava (a starchy root) produced in Colombia.

The exportation of illegal drugs has become a multibillion-dollar industry for Colombia's underground economy; some of this money has been cycled into the national economy, particularly into construction. Colombia's geographic location near the Caribbean has made it a center for contraband since the colonial period. Historically, much of the contraband has been shipped through Panama. With respect to drugs, Colombia was a source of marijuana cultivated on the Guajira Peninsula in the later 1960s. Cocaine was the principal illegal export in the 1970s and 1980s; in the 1990s, heroine has become increasingly important.

The two cartels most responsible for the international drug trade have been those of Medellín and Cali. The Medellín group had humble origins as small-time importers of contraband and exporters of marijuana in the late 1960s and 1970s. By the late 1970s, however, they had organized massive and elaborate international networks to export cocaine. In the late 1980s and early 1990s, they were responsible for widespread bombings and kidnappings in Colombia. García Márquez has written a journalistic account of these kidnappings, *Noticia de un secuestro* (*News of a Kidnapping*, 1996).

The cartel of Cali was created by individuals with business and banking backgrounds, and has not engaged in the violence associated with the Medellín group. Both cartels have been weakened in the 1990s with the arrests and deaths of many of their leaders, including Pablo Escobar from Medellín, who was first arrested, later escaped, and eventually killed by the Colombian police. Despite these defeats, cocaine and heroine trade remain multibillion-dollar operations into the turn of the century.

2

Religion

Organized religion plays a key role in many facets of Colombian society and culture, even more than in most other Latin American countries. The Roman Catholic Church, which has enjoyed a privileged status in the state during most of Colombia's history, has been a dominant force in religious life, and often a significant force in other areas of Colombian life and society. It has overshadowed the efforts of Protestant churches, which have always had a minor role in Colombian life. Even the drug lords of the 1980s claimed to be fervent Catholics, and several were known to attend Catholic mass regularly. So deeply does Catholic religion and culture permeate Colombian life that Nobel Laureate Gabriel García Márquez has suggested in one novel that the only difference between conservatives and liberals in Colombia is that the conservatives go to mass earlier. Indeed, more than 95 percent of Colombians, whatever their political persuasions may be, are baptized Catholics. Today, Colombians tend to feel that it is their role to uphold the tradition of the Catholic Church in Latin America. The Roman Catholic Church in Colombia is widely recognized as one of the most conservative in Latin America and has not played an important role in the political sphere when change has been needed. Liberal and radical elements of the Catholic Church do exist in Colombia, but their real effect has always been minimal in this bastion of conservative theology and religious practice.

The church has always had its critics in Colombia, too. Historically, the Liberal Party has always favored limiting the enormous wealth and political influence of the church; several of Colombia's civil wars have been attempts to resolve the ongoing conflict in Colombia over the proper role of the church.

Some of the nation's most recognized intellectuals, from José María Vargas Vila to Gabriel García Márquez and Gustavo Alvarez Gardeazábal, in fact, have been critics of the Roman Catholic Church in Colombia (see chapters 6 and 7).

HISTORICAL BACKGROUND

With the conquest of the region in the sixteenth century, the Spaniards began a process of evangelization among the Indians and institutionalization of the Roman Catholic Church. Religious zeal was at a zenith in Spain during the period of the conquest and colonization of the Americas; the evangelization of this region was a high priority for the colonial government.

The Roman Catholic Church was central to virtually all facets of life—including the political, educational, and economic—in New Granada during the three centuries of Spanish colonial rule, during which the church established a firm and lasting place in Colombian society. The Spanish monarchy created the close bond between church and state. Colombia was a relatively important ecclesiastical center in the colonial period; it was one of the few colonies to have a bishop who served as viceroy.

Education was one of the church's most important spheres of activity; religious orders founded most of Colombia's schools and universities. The Jesuits were particularly active, founding the Pontificia Universidad Javeriana in 1622, but were expelled from Colombia (and the remainder of Latin America) in the 1760s. Before their demise, however, they left their mark, establishing the first printing presses and editing the first books.

The church became an economic force in the colonial period by receiving large land grants from the Spanish government, becoming the owners of approximately one third of the nation's territory. With these holdings, as well as other substantive sources of wealth, the church played a powerful role in political decision making in the colonial period, continuing this role after the independence in the nineteenth century.

The Constitution of 1886 and the Concordat of 1887 institutionalized the church's long-standing role in Colombia. The constitution stated clearly that "the Apostolic and Roman Catholic religion is that of the nation." Consequently, there was a widespread acceptance of the idea that the church should be protected and respected. This constitution also protected the freedom of worship to "all sects not contrary to Christian morality or law." The Concordat of 1887 confirmed the church's essential role in key aspects of Colombian life: birth, education, marriage, and death were all areas in which the church had an official function. Some political forces were opposed to the concordat, pointing out that its stipulations contradicted the constitution.

Conservative victories in the nineteenth-century civil wars assured that the church remained a powerful force in Colombian political and economic life in the late nineteenth and early twentieth centuries. From 1887 to 1930, the church prospered under conservative rule and consistently supported the party's candidates and political positions. This privileged and comfortable status lasted well into the twentieth century.

During much of the twentieth century, there has been intense debate and conflict in Colombia over the exact role of the Roman Catholic Church and the clergy. The 1950s civil war, identified as La Violencia, marked a crucial period in the history of the church in Colombia. The violence that began with the assassination of popular liberal leader Jorge Eliécer Gaitán quickly expanded into widespread anticonservative, anticlerical, and antigovernment acts. The next presidential election was won by a leader of the most conservative and traditionally Catholic wing of the Conservative Party, Laureano Gómez. He intensified the violence with the objective of "purifying" the nation. The eventual solution to the conflicts of La Violencia was the pact of the National Front, the 1958 agreement between the two traditional political parties. When the Catholic priest Camilo Torres returned from Louvain to Colombia in 1959, this was the situation he encountered.

The Roman Catholic Church lost some of its power and much of its prestige during the years of La Violencia. In the late nineteenth and early twentieth centuries, the church had prospered under conservative rule and provided full support for conservative candidates. When the liberals came into power in 1930, historical conflicts over church privilege were reopened, and the role of the church as central to national life was seriously threatened. With conflicts of La Violencia, the church responded by identifying the cause of religion with the Conservative Party and condemning the liberals as atheists and communists. During the 1950s, priests and church leaders became political activists in favor of the Conservative Party, mobilizing their flocks against all liberals and even handing out Conservative Party ballots in parish offices.

With the end of La Violencia in the form of the truce agreements of the National Front, a consensus developed in the church hierarchy that the church ought to remain distant from partisan political activity. The church recognized that the two main parties needed to coexist in Colombia, and thus blessed the formation of the National Front. With this new attitude, the church hierarchy also changed its focus, turning to strengthening its own institutions. New dioceses, parishes, bureaucracies, and centers of study were created. Social programs and religious outreach were, once again, an important focus of the new institutional programs, which led to a renewed self-reliance and less dependence on secular interests.

In 1944, the Roman Catholic Church in Europe established Catholic Social Action, or Catholic Action, thus forming a group of programs for social and educational development. As the local hierarchy in Colombia gradually adopted the idea of Catholic Action, they accepted implicitly—for the very first time—the concept of social change as a desirable national goal. Catholic Action in Colombia attempted to offer a new direction for the Colombian political system by designing a "Roman" emphasis for the nation's modernization process. Among the loose collection of programs operated under the aegis of Catholic Action were ones to support trade union movements and for establishment of radio schools for peasants.

Different groups of religious leaders, each working independently, developed the pioneer programs of Catholic Action, and these disparate progams were later united. A parish priest, Father Salcedo, founded a radio school program, Acción Cultural Popular (ACPO), in the rural village of Sutatenza; after it was successful in several small communities, it was incorporated into the agenda of Catholic Action (see chapter 4). It became a widespread method for educating peasants in rural areas, financed primarily by the church, but it did receive some support from the United Nations Educational, Scientific, and Cultural Organization (UNESCO). The broadcasts of this radio school program consisted of a combination of music, news, reading, writing and mathematics skills, domestic skills, and religious programs. ACPO also published a weekly magazine, *El Campesino*, to accompany the broadcasts.

Similarly, in 1946, the Jesuits founded the Unión de Trabajadores de Colombia (UTC), which soon became Colombia's largest trade union. Originally organized as a counterbalance to the leftist-oriented Confederation of Colombian Workers (Confederación de Trabajadores Colombianos, or CTC), by the late 1960s, it had become the larger of the two. By the 1970s, the church was providing only 5 to 10 percent of the total UTC budget, and the role of priests was less in supervision than in providing moral advice. In the 1960s, the church was active in supporting the efforts of peasants to obtain land, and it supported the Agrarian Reform Law of 1961.

Father Camilo Torres, nevertheless, was highly critical of the church's efforts to reform. He argued that the church lacked the financial resources to achieve substantive economic development and widespread improvement of the lives of the peasants. After 1964, his critique became increasingly strident and visible in Colombia. By the mid–1960s, he was condemning the church's hierarchy for not actively supporting a revolutionary overthrow of the government. Needless to say, Torres's program and pronouncement sent shock waves throughout the church and Colombian society at large. Church officials refused to recognize the validity of any of Torres's arguments, for they contradicted the institutionalized strategy of progressive development through the programs of Catholic Action. Torres proposed a return to direct clerical participation in the political process, a position already rejected by Catholic Action.

In 1965, Father Torres announced the formation of a new political coalition, the Frente Unido, which he conceived as a revolutionary popular movement willing to accept the support of any other truly revolutionary groups. After separating himself from the church, Torres became a soldier in the Army of National Liberation and appeared in a variety of public forums to promote the ideas of the Frente Unido. He was killed in combat with government soldiers on February 15, 1966.

The leftist challenges to Catholic Action as a developmental strategy, carried out by Father Camilo Torres and other revolutionary armed groups, have been largely ineffectual in Colombia. Their plans for action have been generally rejected, not only by the major political parties, but also by the media and the majority of the citizenry. Nevertheless, the very rise of such revolutionary and armed groups attests to the flaws and failures of Catholic Action as a developmental strategy. The church's inability to maintain Catholic Action as a viable developmental institution in response to modernization in Colombia can be attributed to weaknesses in the Colombian church's social doctrine and in its organizational structure. Catholic Action arose from documents that were conceived in a very general and abstract fashion, lacking the necessary specific details for carrying out an effective developmental strategy.

The role of the church was modified in 1973, when President Misael Pastrana and church officials signed a new concordat. It modified the church as the official state religion, yet still affirmed that "Roman Catholicism is the religion of the great majority of Colombians." It also confirmed the pope's right to name bishops of Colombian nationality, the independence of the church from civil powers, and the removal of tax-exempt status for church properties.

Three other issues were the cause of a national debate in Colombia: the mission territories, education, and marriage. In isolated rural areas populated by Indians, the church had a long-standing priority over the government to educate and provide social services in these mission territories. With this concordat, the church's network of schools and social services was to be transferred gradually to the state. The teaching of Catholicism had been required in all Colombian educational institutions, and this requirement was abolished with the 1973 concordat. This concordat also provided for civil marriages outside of the church.

Since the 1940s, there has been a gradual change in church activity, modifying its conservative positions and placing increasingly more emphasis on the temporal. The Colombian Catholic Church has been in a process of transformation, but has been doing so at a pace much slower than the remainder of Latin America. The process of modernization originally promoted by the series of liberal governments from 1930 to 1946 was the initial reason for many of the changes. Doctrinal changes made by Popes John XXIII and Paul VI, and the church hierarchy in Rome have also required changes in Colombia.

Beginning in the 1940s, there has been an ideological split within the church in Colombia, a division between social conservatives and social reformers. This division was exacerbated by changes in directives from Rome in the late 1950s and 1960s. Popes John XXIII and Paul VI issued a series of encyclicals intended to modernize the church and, above all, to change its role in society. These new pronouncements underlined the state's responsibility to eradicate or reduce socioeconomic inequalities. At the same time, they emphasized the role of the church in spearheading these reforms. The conservative Colombian church hierarchy—which many scholars consider the most conservative in Latin America—tended to ignore these encyclicals until the 1968 Consejo Episcopal Latinoamericano (CELAM) conference in Medellín.

This conference pointed to the serious social and economic implications of class differences, the urgent need for reforms of basic institutions in Colombia and Latin America, and social action and political activism as methods for spreading Christianity throughout the world. These proposed changes received the same unenthusiastic reception among Colombian bishops and other church authorities as the proposals of the revolutionary priest Camilo Torres. Review of these reactions indicate that the conservatism and isolation of the Colombian episcopate have been continued because of career patterns in education and church administration—with little or no experience dealing with social issues or any other real-world problems.

THE ROMAN CATHOLIC CHURCH TODAY

With respect to size, Colombia's clergy and church organizations compare favorably with those of other Latin American nations. Differences over political matters, limited economic resources, and relatively weak training of priests, however, have limited the church's organizational power.

Today, the vast majority of Colombians are Catholics more in name than in practice. They are particularly attentive to the formal aspects of Catholicism, dutifully returning to the church for life's milestones: birth, baptism, first communion, marriage, and death. The Catholic religion is perceived as a part of cultural heritage; religious practices have relatively little importance in personal and business life. Still, masses are relatively well attended in the urban areas, particularly by women.

Women seem to take the practice of religion more seriously than men: church attendance has traditionally been associated with virtue among women. The influence of the church and the participation of the populace also varies greatly by region. The Antioquians and the citizens of Popayán are generally recognized as being particularly devout. In Popayán, the observance of religious holidays, especially during Holy Week, is recognized as the most elaborate, well-prepared, and enthusiastically attended in the nation.

The details of how religion is practiced in Colombia also vary slightly according to social class. Religious practices among uneducated peasants are quite different from the more educated upper classes. In some rural areas, folk religions affect the practice of Catholicism. Syncretism involves Catholic beliefs blending with indigenous and African religious practices. Generally speaking, these syncretic Catholic religious practices are based on a very limited training in Catholicism. Peasants tend to seek aid from the church to protect them from supernatural punishment. The saints are believed to be more accessible to God and willing, under the right circumstances, to intervene for the welfare of the individual or collective causes. Consequently, the Virgin Mary and one's patron saint are regarded with deep reverence. Natural disasters are believed to be sent by God; peasants often believe that the events of life—even epidemics—are entirely dependent on God's will. The church and the government have initiated programs in the second half of this century to change some of these attitudes and encourage peasants to take a more proactive role in defining their social and economic lives.

Well-educated, elite social groups in Colombia often have close personal relations with the upper echelon of the church hierarchy. The clergy and church authorities tend to be of upper-class origins, and thus share common interests with Colombia's oligarchy. These same political and social elite provide the largest part of the membership in lay religious organizations and support the Catholic Church with financial contributions.

Although Catholic religious practices may not dominate the personal daily lives of Colombians, many scholars consider the influence of the church in some Colombian institutions to be the most pervasive in the Western Hemisphere.[1] This influence resides in politics, education, social welfare systems, and the labor movement. Some of this influence involves church-financed programs; much more power is wielded informally through interpersonal relations and unwritten custom.

The ratio of priests to inhabitants in Colombia has been one of the highest in Latin America—approximately one to four thousand in the 1970s, with that figure declining slightly over the past thirty years. In recent decades, more than thirty religious communities for men have been in operation in Colombia. The three largest—Christian Brothers, the Jesuits, and the Salesians—have specialized almost exclusively in education. There have been more than eighty religious communities for women, the largest being La Congregación de las Hermanas de la Caridad Dominicanas de la Presentación de la Santísima Virgen de Tours (the Congregation of Dominican Sisters of Charity of the Presentation of the Very Holy Virgin of Tours). Some of these communities are of Spanish and French origin, but more than one-fourth of the orders are Colombian.

Despite official efforts to establish distance between the church and state, relations have been closer than in any other Latin American nation. The church is involved in the rituals of daily life and, most importantly with respect to political power, in the rituals of government acts. The church is regularly called upon to offer its blessing for official acts at the highest levels, and often appears at the lower levels, too—giving its blessing for new government programs and works. Most public dedication ceremonies are still conducted with at least one member of the clergy on the sight.

The Colombian Catholic Church has attempted to distance itself from the Conservative Party. Nevertheless, the long-standing ties between the two groups remain, both de facto and in the public perception. Despite this role in partisan politics, there is a generalized perception among the populace that the Roman Catholic Church in Colombia remains aloof to real social problems, that it does not reach the population effectively, and a growing number of priests believe the lack of action on the part of the episcopate implies support for an unjust social and political system. The national effort at development has been limited because the impact of the church on reform remains piecemeal and apparently not reflective of an ongoing commitment.

OTHER INSTITUTIONAL RELIGIONS

The Roman Catholic Church has lost its official status as the state religion in Colombia. More than any other Latin American nation, however, Catholicism is the de facto state religion today as much as it was in 1887, when the Colombian constitution declared it the official religion. Consequently, Protestant and non-Christian religions have had relatively little historical presence in Colombia. A small minority of Colombians, mostly European immigrants who have settled in Colombia this century, have discretely attended Protestant churches, such as the Anglican Church or the Lutheran Church. Small Protestant services are also held for foreigners, such as diplomats or businesspeople. There is also a relatively small Jewish population in Colombia that still practices Judaism.

Evangelical religious missions from the United States have also arrived in Colombia over recent decades. In general, they have been significantly less successful with the populace than in some other Latin American countries. Since the 1980s, however, some of these evangelical groups have made inroads in working-class neighborhoods of urban areas. They have made enough progress, in fact, to appear as a right-wing Christian political force in Colombia, although their real political influence in the 1990s has been negligible.

3

Social Customs and Daily Life

Colombians are great enthusiasts of formal social customs and are highly regionalistic in their methods of living social life. Their regional customs are invariably rural, usually with origins in colonial and nineteenth-century life, which Colombians have idealized considerably and tend to view with nostalgia. These origins can be traced back to Spanish, indigenous, and African traditions. For many Colombians, the "real" Colombia is this traditional and rural *Colombia linda* (beautiful Colombia), populated by hard-working peasants dressed in regional costumes, dancing traditional folkloric dances, enjoying traditional foods and festivities.

Although traditional rural life has persisted to some degree in Colombia—regional festivals are still organized and regional cuisine is still prepared—the modernization process since the 1930s, the mass migration to the urban areas since the 1950s, and the rise of the illicit drug trade since the 1980s have all radically altered the traditional concepts of *Colombia linda*. The increase of street violence and brusque entrance of postmodern life in Colombia seem to have caused a reaction in some sectors of Colombian society, sectors that turn increasingly to an idealized past as a way of dealing with the present. For example, the capital city of Bogotá was recently renamed "Santa Fé de Bogotá," thus evoking its colonial past.

The one Colombian writer who has most masterfully captured the essence of traditional rural life and peasant customs is fiction writer Tomás Carrasquilla, a storyteller from Antioquia (see Chapter 6). Carrasquilla's idealized evocations of life on farms and plantations in Antioquia were always nostalgic in tone. His use of an oral storyteller's methods make his stories particularly ef-

Village life in western valley

fective in transporting twentieth-century readers back to a time when life was supposedly—at least in Carrasquilla's fictionalized version of things much more simple, healthy, and pleasant.

Other than the Spanish language, the most influential factor in the unifying of Colombian culture and customs is the Catholic Church. The Mass, religious observances, and objects of religious veneration are elements of a common culture that most Colombians share, no matter what their regional or class origins may be. Holy Day celebrations, particularly those days honoring a community's patron saint, are events of great importance for the social cohesion that unites members of the community in a common bond. The Holy Week processions of Popayán and Tunja and the celebration of the Corpus Christi festival in Bogotá are among the largest and most spectacular in the country. Indeed, the increasingly notable political crises and deterioration of the social fiber of Colombia undoubtedly have some relationship with the loss of power and prestige of the Catholic Church in the second half of the century.

Colombians celebrate many of their customs regionally or in their villages of origin; indeed, many urban Colombians still return to their home villages (or their parents' home villages) on certain holidays to celebrate the *fiestas*. Several special events, however, virtually paralyze the entire nation, the most important of which is the *Reinado de Belleza*, the national beauty contest held in Cartagena each December. Equally important is the *Mundial de Fútbol*—the World Cup in soccer. The vast majority of Colombians interrupt their normal social and work routines in order to watch the *Reinado* and the *Mundial* on television; of course, they are the main topic of social intercourse for several days (or even weeks) leading up to the final event. Those occasions when the pope visits Colombia, are also events that virtually paralyze normal work and social routines, as many Colombians attempt to follow the pope's movements and words in Colombia on a minute-by-minute basis on radio and television.

DRESS AND TRADITIONAL COSTUMES

The clothing worn by professionals and middle- to upper-class sectors in urban areas is basically the same that would be found in any urban area of the United States and Europe.[1] Much of the finest clothing worn by men and women in Colombia is, in fact, imported from the United States and Europe, although Colombia does have an active textile industry and produces clothing and shoes similar to those purchased abroad. Until the 1990s, styles for both sexes tended to be more conservative, particularly in Bogotá, where dark colors were preferred and professional men tended to wear classic black or grey suits. Generally speaking, Colombians in urban areas prefer to dress with as much elegance as possible, to such an extent that men from Bogotá are frequently the object of ridicule by Colombians from other regions, who tend to consider the *bogotanos* excessively refined in their tastes.

Clothing in rural areas tends to be far less elegant, usually for use both at home and in the fields, and often made at home. In these areas, men tend to wear loose-fitting pants, and women wear loose-fitting skirts. Both cover themselves with different kinds of cloaks, depending on the region and temperature, the most traditional of which is the *ruana*, worn draped over the shoulders. These cloaks, which are made of wool in regions of cold climate, may also serve as blankets at night. Peasants construct different types of sandals for footwear, but often work in the fields barefooted.

Colombians have preserved the tradition of certain regional clothing that is basically the "elegant" version of peasant clothing used only to celebrate holidays, frequently for the purpose of dancing traditional local dances. Typical traditional dress from the interior highland region (a man's costume from Boyacá) consisted of: trousers of striped material without a waistband; a diagonally striped, open-necked, buttonless shirt of linen or flannel, depending on the climate; a hat with a silk braid and a black band; and embroidered leather sandals with light linen toe caps. Occasionally, they carried a piece of cloak (*manta*) on their shoulders. The traditional costume of women from neaby Tolima consisted of skirts of simple, ordinary linen and a blouse of white cambric or ba-

Traditional highland clothing

tiste, with a round, low neck and balloon sleeves decorated with hand-embroidered tapes or braids. They wore a shawl over the shoulders for decoration and protection from insects. which was made from gingham, a very popular imported cloth in the nineteenth century, brought by ships up the Magdalena River. They also wore a mantilla of a velvet-like cloth known as *fula*, topped off with a Suaza hat (typical hat of this region). Their earrings were of gold from nearby mines.

The clothing of the typical mule-driving peasant from Antioquia, on the other hand, was more hearty. His clothing consisted of homespun trousers of unbleached cloth when they were plain, or of striped blanket material when stripes were preferred. He wore them turned up (even when he was not working), for his work demanded it: He had to wade across rivers and swamps. He typically wore a long-sleeved T-shirt, without a collar and made of white flannel with red stripes. This type of peasant was famous for his leather pouch, which was full of useful tools, and worn crosswise on the right side. Country women from Antioquia often wore a skirt with numerous tucks and folds, held by a waistband which was tied, made from brightly colored printed fabrics, such as chintz or calico. The impeccable blouses were low-necked and had loose-fitting sleeves with Barcelona lace and starched-lace cuffs with ribbons. They wore head scarfs made of merino wool for cold climates and of serge for the warmer ones.

Typical traditional clothing was quite different in the Caribbean coastal region. In general, men wore long, loose-fitting flowery shirts called *guayaberas*. Caribbean fishermen typically wore white cotton trousers gathered behind at the waist. Shirts (*chupas*) were loose and long, and worn outside the trousers. They often carried a machete, a colored knapsack, and wore a handkerchief at the neck. Traditional women's clothing was simple, often made of plain-colored cotton, frequently printed with bright colors, with much use of red and contrasting colors. They wore a handkerchief on the head, knotting it in a variety of ways.

NATIONAL AND REGIONAL FESTIVITIES

Colombia has numerous national holidays, most of which are planned to coincide with a weekend to create a *puente*, so that Colombians can enjoy a three-day weekend with some frequency. In a staunchly Catholic country such as Colombia, obviously the major dates on the Christian calendar, such as Christmas and Easter, are important national holidays. Nevertheless, many of the most typical and well-known celebrations are regional events that, in some cases, have a tradition of several centuries.

Feminine beauty is highly prized in Colombia, perhaps more visibly so than in any other Western nation. The most important national scenario for the matter of feminine beauty to be played out is the annual *Reinado de Belleza*. During the year leading up to the final competition in Cartagena, regional beauty queens are selected from each of Colombia's departments. The regional competitions in themselves are important events, with ample press coverage that usually includes the frequent appearance of color pictures of the beauty queen candidates in all Colombian newspapers. By November, Colombians across the nation are well acquainted with the visual images of the top candidates, and engage in endless discussions of their different qualities. By the time the event appears on national television, transmitted live from Cartagena, the Colombian public is as affixed to their television sets as Americans are for the Superbowl or the French for the Tour de France. In addition to this regional and national competition, there are numerous other beauty contests throughout the year in Colombia, usually associated with a local celebration.

So pervasive are these beauty contests that several Colombian social commentators have studied this phenomenon, demonstrating that there is a crowning of a new beauty queen in Colombia on an average of once a week. García Márquez satirizes Colombian beauty queens in his story, "Big Mama's Funeral," in a passage in which he ridicules several of Colombia's national institutions.

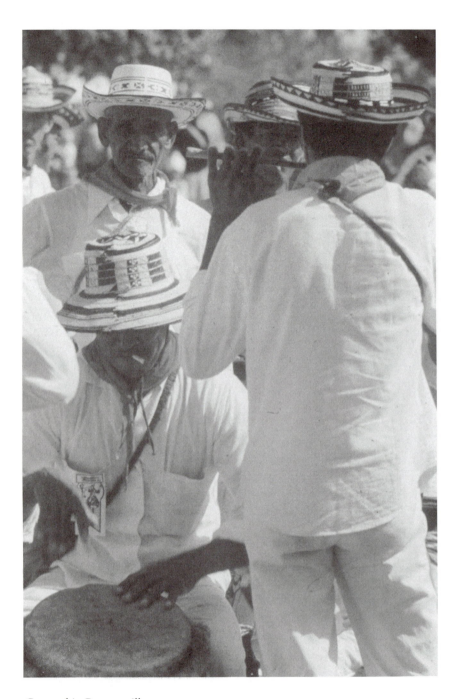

Carnaval in Barranquilla

Carnaval masks, Barranquilla

Beyond religious holidays and the national beauty contest, the remaining festivities tend to be regional or local celebrations. The annual Carnaval of Barranquilla is one of the largest traditional celebrations—the Colombian version of the carnaval in Brazil. There are many other local festivities similar to Carnaval, only smaller in dimension. Some of these festivities are quite unique to the specific region, such as the Festival of the Devil in the town of Riosucio in the department of Caldas.

TRADITIONAL AND REGIONAL DANCE

In general, traditional dances have the same name as the most typical music of each region (see chapter 8). That is, *bambuco* music of the interior highland is also danced as the *bambuco*. Other traditional dances from the interior highland region are the *guabina* and the *torbellino*. Traditional dances from the Caribbean coast are the *cumbia*, the *mapalé*, and the *bullerengue*. The *currulao* is one of the most typical dances from the greater Cauca region.

The *bambuco* has folk origins, but the way it is danced today has both a rural and an urban variant, as well as certain regional variations, for the *bambuco* has been adapted in regions other than the interior highland. In all cases, the dance steps are simple and elegant, movements are withdrawn, and contact between the couple dancing is fleeting and delicate. The dance is based exclusively on the delicate steps—there is no visible emotion, and certainly no lifting of the partner. Technically speaking, the *bambuco* has an eight-part structure: invitation, eights, elbows, flirting, man chasing, woman chasing, kneeling down, and embrace.

The *guabina* generally has little fixed structure, either in its music or the way it is danced; this dance leaves considerable room for improvisation. In all of its variants, women play a major role in the singing, and all the participants alternate between singing and dancing. For Colombians, the "purest" form of the *guabina* is danced in the villages of Vélez and Chiquinquirá, both located in the interior highland. In its structured forms, the *guabina* has eight parts: introduction, flirting, little steps, pivoting, caresses, *cepillao* in circle, handkerchief game, and exit.

The *torbellino* is a close relative to the *bambuco*, and could well have indigenous origins, but today is considered a *mestizo* dance, i.e., a mixture of Spanish and Indian influences. Originally danced during pilgrimages, it is danced with few instruments. It is even more restrained than the *bambuco*; the couples do not hold hands or even touch each other at all. A distanced and discreet flirting is maintained. The general movement and intention of the *torbellino* is a faithful copy of a whirlwind, which is where it gets its name. The formal structure of the *torbellino* is as follows: invitation, eights facing, chasing, eights back-to-back, man chasing, crossing, spiral, and exit.

Typical dances from the Caribbean coast are quite different in intention and form, with considerably more visible body expression and overt sexuality. With African and Native American origins, the *cumbia* is an expression of free and open form. Its open eroticism and sexuality were in direct opposition to the church and the highly controlled dancing forms that came from Spain and the interior highland region. In the *cumbia*, the woman dances freely while the man follows her and attempts to grasp her at the waist; in order to do so, he bends down and moves around her. Body movement encourages contact. The *bullerengue* is closely related to the *cumbia*, with clear African origins. It is a women's dance, a ritual celebration of puberty which exalts the initiation of young girls. It is danced to the rhythm of palms and drums, with a well-defined form: the young girls come out in line, singing together and clapping, with their hands held high, marking the beat with very short steps like those of the *cumbia*. The formal structure of the *bullerengue* is as follows: invitation, corridor, circles, crossing, circles, and exit.

Not much material support is needed for the *mapalé*: two drums, one known as the *llamador* (caller) and the other, the *tambor mayor* (main drum). The *mapalé*, like the *cumbia* and the *bullerengue*, is of African origin. It is a song to Eros, with great emphasis on erotic physical movement. According to accounts from the sixteenth and seventeenth centuries, the *mapalé* was originally danced in lines, and then in circles, with the dancers carrying torches. The structure of the *mapalé* is as follows: invitation, man circles, free dance, the arms game, round, crossing, free dances, and exit.

The *currulao* holds roughly the same privileged status in greater Cauca as the *bambuco* holds in the interior highland: It is the model for much of the traditional dance in the western area of Colombia. Studies indicate that the word *currulao* comes from a drum called the *cununo*. Historically, the *currulao* has been considered so sensual and wild that it has been banned during several periods of Colombia's history. In the nineteenth century, when this dance was developed, it included jumps forward and back, as well as brusque turns and jumps, with plenty of waving of skirts and handkerchiefs. Unlike the *cumbia* and some of the erotic dances from the Caribbean coast, however, the *currulao* is danced with sobriety—as if it were a task. Some scholars believe it was originally a ritual dance of conquest, even though it is sometimes danced with some emotion and eroticism.[2]

FOOD CONSUMPTION AND REGIONAL CUISINE

Most middle and upper-middle class Colombians prepare and eat relatively elaborate meals that reflect Spanish and indigenous gastronomic traditions. Unlike in Mexico and some other parts of Latin America, Colombian food is not prepared with the "hot" spices that foreigners frequently associate with Latin American cuisine. Rather, the typical meal of the upper sectors of Colombian society consists of a fresh fruit dish, a homemade soup of some kind, and a main dish with meat or fish accompanied by rice and/or potatoes. (Spices and peppers are usually added as an extra condiment, according to individual taste.) The meal usually ends with a sweet of very high sugar content. Colombians normally start the day with a light breakfast, have a substantive lunch at midday, and a slightly lighter dinner in the early evening. Lunch and dinner tend to consist of a diet such as that described above. The lower-income sectors generally do not have the luxury of meat or fish, and eat a more carbohydrate-rich diet. When these families have a dessert, it is frequently made from *panela*, a brown sugar readily available and produced in Colombia—its per capita consumption of sugar is one of the highest in Latin America.

On special occasions or at restaurants, Colombians prepare one of their numerous specialty dishes, such as *ajiaco* (a stew with three types of potato, chicken, and corn, served with capers and cream, and avocado as an accompaniment) or *sobrebarriga* (a type of flank steak marinated in a special sauce), both specialties of the interior highland region. Gourmet cooks in Bogotá also serve *cuchuco*, prepared from wheat grits and pork. In the region of Antioquia, a special dish is *mondongo*—tripe. In the Caribbean coastal region, the most typical dish is *arroz con coco*, a rice dish cooked in coconut oil. Another special dish from the Caribbean region is a fish or chicken stew called *sancocho*. In many parts of Colombia, the traditional dessert is *manjar blanco*, which is sweet milk curds.

Colombians consume high quantities of beer and coffee and relatively little milk and wine. Colombia has been producing its own beer and coffee since the late nineteenth century. Its beer and soft drink industries are quite large and mostly locally owned (with the exception of Coca Cola, which is consumed in great quantities in Colombia). Colombian wine is of low quality and production; most Colombians who desire wine purchase either (economical) Chilean wine or (expensive) French imports. Colombia also produces a local rum and a kind of corn or sugar brandy called *aguardiente*. On social occasions such as cocktail parties, Colombians who do not drink beer can usually be seen ordering (expensive) American whiskey or (inexpensive) Colombian *aguardiente*.

Colombians who can afford the luxury participate in a unique coffee culture comparable in some ways to the coffee revolution in the United States over the past decade. Traditionally, Colombians have ordered their coffee either as *tinto* (black coffee, generally stronger than American coffee, but not espresso) or *café* (coffee with warm milk, usually consumed with breakfast). Colombians also order their coffee as *perico* (small cup of coffee with a dash of milk). With the rise of elegant coffee shops (located in the most chic urban areas of the major cities), Colombians order either one of the three above or espresso, capuccino, or similar coffee drinks. In most public and private offices, the first order of business is to offer a visitor either a *tinto* or *agua aromática* (a type of herbal tea). Coffee culture also includes a combination with the Colombians' other passion—literature—giving rise to the coffee house/bookstore (*café/librería*) which allows customers to simply consume caffeine and books, or offer poetry readings and book signings. Even some bars in Colombia have had organized poetry readings in the 1980s and 1990s.

The same comfortable Colombians who participate in the exclusive coffee culture can enjoy an entire gamut of national or international cuisine that has become widespread in the major cities over the past three decades. Consequently, residents of Bogotá can easily locate restaurants serving the *bandeja paisa* from Antioquia, seafood from the coastal areas, or the cuisines of Mexico or Europe. Since the 1980s, in fact, Colombians have even opened vegetarian restaurants and sushi bars, which would have been an anomaly in the more traditional nation of predominately Colombian and Spanish traditions.

Official estimates vary considerably concerning the quantity and quality of the average diet in Colombia, but there is a general agreement that the average calorie and protein intake for the population at large has been slightly inadequate since the 1950s. Different studies point to an average intake of two thousand to twenty-five hundred calories (depending on the period and region studied). The dietary inadequacy has been a consequence of the fact that the population has grown more rapidly than food production, a problem that has been made more acute by certain cultural attitudes. More specifically, lower-income Colombians and peasants generally eschew eggs, milk, fruit, and vegetable and fish products (all of which are produced in Colombia), preferring a diet high in carbohydrates and meat.

SPORTS

Colombia is typical of Latin America with its participation in and observance of sports, but with some slight variations. The city of Cali is the setting for a high level of participatory sports, where men and women alike are active joggers, cyclists, volleyball players, and are even involved in softball leagues. Professional soccer, bicycling, and boxing are three sports typically adopted by working-class Colombians who, if they are successful, can use them for social and economic improvements that would otherwise be unlikely to attain.

As in all of Latin America, Colombia's principal passion is *fútbol* (soccer). Professional soccer was founded in Colombia in 1948, after a players' strike in Argentina made it feasible to contract some of that nation's stars, such as Alfredo Distefano, who held virtually mythical status in Colombia. Colombians can be as fanatical about soccer as their well-known counterparts in Brazil and Great Britain. Most Colombian men and many women become fans of their professional team at an early age and remain loyal for a lifetime. Soccer is the most popular sport in Colombia, where there are sixteen teams that belong to a professional league and compete for the annual championship. There is also a lower-level semiprofessional league for training potential soccer players. Professional soccer matches are scheduled for Sunday afternoons and occasionally Wednesday evenings. Colombian teams have generally competed well on the international scene since the early 1980s, although usually falling short in championship matches with teams from Argentina, Brazil, or Mexico. In the late 1980s and early 1990s, a massive influx of capital from drug cartels allowed some Colombian professional teams to improve markedly by contracting some of the most capable players available on the international market—star players that Colombian teams were not generally able to finance until these new sources of funding became available. (It was openly recognized in Colombia that the "América" team from Cali and the "Nacional" team from Medellín were highly financed by drug operators; for a while, the "Millonarios" team from Bogotá also had connections with drug money.)

Colombia is an exception in Latin America in its interest and support of bicycling; in recent decades, it has been the most prominent Latin American nation in international professional cycling competition. For example, the "Café de Colombia" team has competed successfully in European and North American cycling competitions. Professional cycling arose in Colombia in the 1950s, and its popularity had much to do with the expert transmission of European races over the radio. Support for professional cycling, however, has waned in Colombia in the 1990s.

Cycling is also practiced recreationally by many Colombians. On Sundays and holidays, the main avenue of Bogotá is closed to automobile traffic in order for recreational cyclists to exercise; some of these weekend bikers even climb several thousand feet up the Andean mountains to small villages overlooking Bogotá. Colombia's most accomplished amateur cyclists, for example, ride their bicyles from downtown Bogotá up to a village called La Calera, where they rest and enjoy soft drinks produced in the United States or Colombia. Some bicycles are made in Colombia, but the high-quality road and mountain bikes are imported from Europe and the United States.

Professional boxing is also practiced in Colombia, with most of the boxers coming from the Caribbean coast. They compete in professional matches in Colombia, and a few of the most successful Colombian boxers, such as "Kid" Pambalé, have gained international reputations. As is the case with soccer, working-class Colombians with little opportunity for education or any other method to climb the socioeconomic ladder may pursue boxing.

Colombia is one of the few Latin American countries, along with Mexico and Peru, that still has a professional bullfighting circuit. Bogotá and Medellín have a *plaza de toros* (bullring) for viewing bullfights, and these spaces are filled with fans during bullfighting season. Many of the bullfights are *novilladas*—beginning professionals who are fighting young, inexperienced bulls.

Baseball has a long tradition in Colombia, but almost exclusively on the Caribbean coast. Semiprofessional teams have been in operation in Barranquilla, Cartagena, and the surrounding area for several decades, some years with more organization and success than others. Certainly, Mexico, Cuba, the Dominican Republic, and Venezuela all have more ample amateur and professional baseball leagues. Nevertheless, an occasional athlete from Colombia has managed to make the move into the major leagues in the United States, the most recent example being infielder Edgar Rentería of the 1997 World Champion Florida Marlins. García Márquez and his friends of the "Group of Barranquilla" were fans of both Colombian and American baseball. García Márquez's good friend, Alvaro Cepeda Samudio (author of two books of fiction, see chapter 6), wrote numerous journalistic articles about baseball and was well informed about American baseball of the 1950s.

WOMEN'S ROLES

The situation of women in Colombia is as problematic as in any Western nation but is made more complex by certain factors specific to Colombia, such as the institutional commodification of feminine beauty. In anticipation of the Juegos del Pacífico in Cali in 1998, for example, one local newspaper described this international athletic event as an opportunity for Cali to show off *la belleza de la mujer caleña* (the beauty of women from Cali). Such comments, which could well upset feminist readers in the United States or Europe, go by unnoticed in Colombia.

The ideal for the successful beauty queen in Colombia is to become a professional model or actress, professions that are quite well paid in Colombia. Angie Cepeda and Sofía Vergara are just two of Colombia's former beauty queens who have become highly successful (Cepeda in modeling and television, Vergara on television). Former Miss Universe Luz Marina Zuluaga enjoyed many years of success on television as a *presentadora* (entertainment show hostess). Paula Turbay (from Bogotá) and Susana Caldas (from the Caribbean coast) are also widely recognized in Colombia for their physical beauty and professional success.

Compared to other Latin American nations, there are relatively few women writers in Colombia; there is, however, a tradition of women writing that dates back to the colonial period and continues through the nineteenth and twentieth centuries. Indeed, one of the most prolific writers of the nineteenth century was Soledad Acosta de Samper. (She was also the first Colombian woman to direct a newspaper.) In the nineteenth and early twentieth centuries, women were the primary *readers* of much of the literature being written. In the 1920s, in fact, one of the most popular organs for distributing literature was a magazine called *La novela semanal*, a publication read primarily by women which published brief novels on a weekly basis. In the midtwentieth century, one of

Colombia's most accomplished novelists was Elisa Mújica. Unfortunately, it seems that being a woman made it quite difficult to gain full credibility as a novelist, although, in general, men and women writers of the period had difficulty maintaining literary careers. Since the 1970s, three of Colombia's most capable professional writers have been women: novelist Albalucía Angel, novelist Fanny Buitrago, and poet María Mercedes Carranza.

To a large degree, the experience and possibilities of women in Colombia is a function of social class. Upper-class Colombian women have been active in politics in recent decades; it is not uncommon for women to hold high-level posts as ministers, for example. Since the presidency of Belisario Betancur in the mid–1980s, it has been common for women to hold these posts. In the middle and lower sectors, however, women are far more limited in their possibilities, and numerous studies point to a high level of abuse of women in the lower classes. Physical abuse of working-class women is particularly acute in Antioquia.

Since the 1980s, an increasing number of women are entering into professions from which they had previously been excluded. For example, there are some women lawyers and physicians in Colombia today. In recent years, women have even broken the barrier in the public sphere of the taxi; it is possible to see an occasional woman driving a taxi in the streets of Bogotá.

URBAN SOCIAL CUSTOMS

Colombian traditions tend to come from rural habits dating back to the colonial period, with some beginning in the nineteenth century. Traditional dances, for example, have roots in the colonial experience, and most reflect a synthesis of sixteenth-century Spanish dance with African and indigenous elements. A few of the dances developed in the nineteenth century. Colombia has become an urban nation, however, since the 1950s, and the majority of the population lives in cities today. (In 1950, two-thirds of the population lived in rural areas; in the late 1990s, approximately three-fourths of Colombia's inhabitants live in cities.) Consequently, new urban customs are arising for the first time. Many of these customs relate to the new rapid-paced urban life, while others can be associated with class structure and the intense patronage involved in urban employment in government jobs.

Social life in urban Colombia is increasingly taking place in private space, to a large extent because of the exceptionally high index of crime and violence on urban streets. In the 1980s and 1990s, therefore, private clubs have mushroomed throughout the major cities. The most elite and traditional private clubs are quite difficult to enter without the proper class credentials and the payment of remarkably high fees. Only the most wealthy individuals whose

Daily life in downtown Cartagena

families have been in the oligarchy for decades find easy access to private clubs such as the Jockey Club, Gun Club, the Country Club, Club de Abogados, Club de Ingenieros, or the Club Médico. Given these limitations, other private clubs with less-strict class restrictions and fees have opened in the last two decades. On Sundays, many middle- and upper middle-class Colombians take their families to these private clubs for meals and recreation.

The new urban life has brought about other changes in the way Colombians interact. Today, urban Colombians are famous for their use and understanding of *la palanca*, which is basically the "in" or "inside track" that one might gain in Colombia because of a personal connection with an individual of power or influence. Most of the many patronage positions gained in Colombia are either a political payback or the result of a *palanca* (a friend or relative helping another Colombian gain a position). Allegiance to political parties and family ties are the source of most *palancas* in Colombia.

Urban Colombians also refer frequently to the *lagarto* (literally, "lizard"), which is basically a social climber who uses any opportunity to gain an advantage by associating with someone higher on the social scale. Consequently, this has a negative connotation in Colombia, and most middle- and upper middle-class Colombians would be ashamed (or outraged) if accused of being a *lagarto*. The term has become so common that there is even a verb used to apply to the act of being a *lagarto*: *lagartear*.

The rigid social structure of Colombia, combined with the highly developed and practiced sense of humor of many of its inhabitants, has produced humorous slang terms for certain typical urban types, such as the *lagarto*. In fact, a Colombian observer has published a book titled *Fauna social colombiana* in which he describes these social types.[3] Thus, the *gallinazo* (vulture) is the term urban Colombians apply to the Don Juan-type who seems to descend on women in virtually any social situation. The *lobo* (wolf), on the other hand, is the lower-class social climber who, despite his efforts to buy his way up the social ladder, is always just a little too vulgar and lacking in refinement. This Colombian "fauna" includes many other social types, and the humor in the terms used is generally based on an understanding of Colombia's rigid social class structure and the refined ways of its traditional elite. Many of the derogatory terms refer to specific types of men and women with lower-class backgrounds.

DRUG CULTURE AND SOCIAL CUSTOMS

From the mid–1980s to the late 1990s, drug culture and drug money have penetrated virtually all sectors of Colombian society, affecting the lives of a vast majority of citizens who have no connections at all with this industry. The rise of drug-trafficking millionaires created a variety of problems in Colombia—including a threat to the traditional social structure that had been in place for centuries.

The founders and leaders of the cartel of Medellín, including figures such as Pablo Escobar, began their dealings as small-time importers of contraband and marijuana in the late 1960s and 1970s. They were of modest, working-class origins. Historically, Colombia has been quite tolerant of contraband, and its two coasts have made it ideal for contraband operators, many of whom have worked through Panama. With this background, they began to construct their international network for exporting cocaine to the United States and Europe, doing so with considerable success by the early 1980s. Once they began surfacing in the social and political scenario in Colombia, they possessed enormous sums of money, but lacked the class credentials to participate successfully in Colombia's closed and conservative upper circles. Pablo Escobar, for example, attempted to participate in Colombian national politics in the early 1980s, and was unsuccessful. Escobar and his working-class cohorts, who possessed more capital than many of Colombia's wealthiest aristocrats, were rejected by the elite families that have fundamentally ruled in Colombia for the past two centuries (longer in some cases).

Escobar contributed huge sums of money (the equivalent of several million dollars) to social service and recreational-type programs in working-class neighborhoods in the poorer outskirts of Medellín.[4] Consequently, he developed an enormous popular following in Medellín and the Antioquia region in general, becoming a figure of mythical and/or legendary proportions. Nevertheless, his substantial wealth and widespread political support in Antioquia were not sufficient for him to be allowed into the social circles of the traditional aristocracy of Medellín or Bogotá. Excluded from the most elite private clubs and churches, he and his cohorts of the cartel of Medellín began purchasing their own private clubs and churches (built and financed by them). By the late 1980s, Colombians were making reference to *narco-curas* ("narco-priests," who were priests paid by the drug traffickers to attend to them) and *narco-poetas* ("narco-poets," who wrote verse in praise of the drug traffickers).

From the United States, drug traffickers such as Pablo Escobar were viewed by U.S. government officials as criminals, which they were. In Colombia, however, the problems with the drug cartels went beyond criminal activity—they shook the very foundation of a social and political structure in place for centuries. With this background, it is possible to understand the eventual alliance between drug traffickers and leftist guerrillas (*narco-guerrillas*); both the working-class drug traffickers and the working-class guerrillas were comprised of individuals who considered themselves excluded from the sociopolitical establishment of Colombia. By the late 1990s, the revolutionary political doctrines of many guerrilla groups were abandoned in favor of this unique alliance between drug traffickers and former political dissidents.

Given the enormous sums of capital available to drug traffickers in Colombia, they have had considerable influence in virtually all spheres of Colombian life, from the social and economic to the political. During the 1980s, Colombia's relative economic health was due, to some extent, to the widespread use of drug money in a variety of legitimate economic activities, particularly the construction of buildings. Consequently, there was a building boom and relative economic stability in Colombia in the 1980s, despite the more uneven economic performance of most other Latin American nations during this period. On the other hand, drug money penetrated everything from the ownership of professional athletic teams to the sponsorship of beauty queens participating in national beauty contests. The campaign and presidency of Ernesto Samper (1994–1998) was tainted by overwhelming evidence that he had received drug money during his campaign, resulting in the most strained relations between the governments of the United States and Colombia since the United States played a role in the independence movement of Panama at the beginning of the century.

4

The Media

In Latin America, as in the remainder of the West, the media are instrumental in shaping the cultural, political, and economic landscape of a nation. In Colombia, this generalization has held true throughout its history, for the development of the nation has been greatly influenced by parallel advancements in the communication media.

The press, which originated in the colonial period of the nation at the end of the eighteenth century, is the oldest of the media. In Colombia, it has traditionally been considered the most credible source of information, due to the prestige associated with the written word. Nonetheless, radio and television have contributed more to the cultural integration of the diverse regions of Colombia than the press did in its first century of existence. Radio emerged in the 1930s, a crucial time of economic growth and development in Colombia, and television was first implemented in the 1950s. Since its inception almost half a century ago, the Colombian television system has made remarkable progress, and its future impact on audiences, due to its audiovisual nature and the rapidly emerging technological advances of the industry in the global context, are increasingly felt in Colombian society at large.

TELEVISION

Television plays a significant role in Colombian life, although it has not been as sophisticated as in some Latin American nations, such as Mexico and Argentina. It has been dominated by governmental control, to varying degrees depending on the political party in power, since its inception in 1954. This control was initially delegated to the Office of Information and Press of the State (Oficina de Información y Prensa del Estado—ODIPE) under the direction of Jorge Luis Arango, who played an essential role in bringing this modern technology to Colombia. The following year, a reorganization of the governing bodies (one of many to follow over the decades) rendered the Televisora Nacional as the new dominating force over television. In spite of its frequent changes in directors, policies, and structure, the organization that has had the most lasting effects on Colombian television is *Inravisión*—the National Institute of Radio and Television (Instituto Nacional de Radio y Televisión)— which basically constitutes a state monopoly of the broadcasting media.

The birth of Colombian television took place under a canopy of dictatorial authority: When Gustavo Rojas Pinilla seized control of the Colombian government by means of a military coup during the tumultuous period of La Violencia, one of his top priorities was the creation of a national television system. He had first seen television in 1936, while on a military trip to Nazi Germany as a major in the army.[1] At that moment, greatly impressed by the innovation in communications, the future dictator conceived the idea of bringing the invention to his homeland. Appointed by Rojas Pinilla, Jorge Luis Arango orchestrated the complex task of acquiring and coordinating the essential equipment, technicians, and skills in a short period of time. Arango's efforts included the collaboration of experts from several foreign countries: the United States, where Fernando Gómez Agudelo, the director of Radiodifusora Nacional, was sent to study the most adequate system of antennas for dealing with Colombia's complex topography; Germany, which possessed the directional antennas required; and Cuba, which had some of the most knowledgeable television technicians in Latin America.

Latin America is a very heterogeneous group of nations with respect to the adoption, development, and management of television. In the 1950s, Cuba, the third Latin American nation to acquire this electronic medium, already had a very sophisticated television system, which was developed in large part by the brothers Goar and Abel Mestre. In fact, in 1948, the Mestre brothers established what was thought to be the world's first twenty-four-hours-a-day news station.[2] The Cuban government, under the dictatorship of Fidel Castro, took over the Mestres' broadcasting system in 1961. Unlike that of Cuba, but similar to the growth of television broadcasting in Colombia, the public sector in Mexico, Peru, and Uruguay provided the initial catalyst in the field, which later was to be opened to private stations. In Argentina and Chile, the ground was broken for television systems by entrepreneurs, and government rival stations followed immediately behind them. In contrast, Costa Rica and Ecuador are characterized by almost complete private ownership.

Despite the skepticism of many Colombians, the inauguration of television in Colombia took place on July 13, 1954, commemorating the first year of Rojas Pinilla's rule. It is estimated that not less than fifteen hundred television sets in the Bogotá area were available to receive the first broadcast, which was transmitted from the basement of the National Library, both beginning and ending with the playing of the Colombian national anthem. In order to facilitate the growth of this nascent medium of communication, the government shortly thereafter subsidized a shipment of fifteen thousand television sets so that the citizens could purchase them at cost. The technical quality of the images transmitted was reported to be excellent, comparable to that of any other nation. Nonetheless, the artistic content of the first televised programs was not found to match the technical quality achieved, and criticism quickly emerged. Before the year's end, the artistic director of Televisora Nacional had already traveled to Argentina to familiarize himself with Argentine theater and to hire young actors and actresses from Buenos Aires.

From television's inception, the Colombian government alluded to the possibility of selling broadcast time to private companies, and in 1955, Televisora Nacional allocated program space to the company Televisión Comercial (TVC), a venture created by the joint forces of two major radio networks, Cadena Radio Colombiana and Radio Cadena Nacional. This initial commercialization of the medium can be seen as one of the starting points of continual controversy among several factions: Televisora Nacional (and later Inravisión), the private television companies, the actors' guild and union, and, of course, the viewers. A few examples of different conflicts throughout the years illustrate this point. In January of 1960, an article from the magazine *Semana* claimed that Televisora Nacional was in a state of crisis due to claims for compensation and written contracts, among other petitions, by the actors' guild, Círculo Colombiano de Actores (CICA). In 1963, the director of Televisora Nacional ordered the suspension of all broadcasting and the closure of the television facilities; this action was attributed to a supposed revision of equipment and adjustments to the programming, but CICA described it as an illegal government strike. Various conflictive elements culminated in the creation of Inravisión, the new administrative body of television in Colombia, at the end of 1963.

The centralized control of Colombian television has affected the exercise of objective programming and the fair offering and selection of tenders in the bidding process. On several occasions, programs have been suspended or even canceled due to their political nature. Politicians regularly used the medium of communication to postulate their political platforms, especially near election time; in fact, in 1990 the thirteen presidential candidates all granted themselves fifteen minutes of free advertising. Another controversial practice that has taken place in Colombian television is the preferential allocation of news broadcasting time to *delfines*, sons and daughters of presidential families who quite often have no professional education in the medium. Such favoritism sometimes extends to certain private companies that are granted broadcasting time in the bidding process when others—sometimes equally worthy—are not. Fernando Restrepo Suárez, a former director of Televisora Nacional (1958–1962), once commented that the technological advances in Colombian television have always been secondary to the political circumstances of the moment, and not, unfortunately, in accordance with the current technology available, the real demands of the country, nor the healthy motor of competition.

In spite of the complications caused by political circumstances, television has progressively made headway in Colombia, integrating modern technology and extending services to more regions. By 1960, only six years after television's arrival, a transmission network of stations already covered almost 80 percent of Colombian territory, and an estimated two million viewers sat in front of the TV screen every night. In 1963, the transmissions reached the Caribbean coastal departments of Atlántico, Bolívar, Córdoba, and Magdalena. Programs in color first illuminated Colombian television screens at the end of the 1970s.

The creation of regional channels was an important milestone for the industry, not only due to its further expansion of the medium, but more importantly for its impelling force towards decentralization. This regional expansion was coupled with the restructuring of Inravisión in 1985, which consisted of the creation of three separate branches: the National Council of Television (Consejo Nacional de Televisión), the Administrative Board (Junta Administrativa), and the Vigilance Committee (Comisión de Vigilancia), each with its respective responsibilities. Regional channels soon to be inaugurated were: Teleantioquia (1985), Telecaribe (1986), Telepacífico (1988), and Telecafé (1992). Cable television, after overcoming some initial obstacles and following the emergence of illegal distribution by pirate companies, was officially approved and implemented in 1987, initially serving twelve thousand subscribers with four basic channels: the sports channel, the Latin channel, the family channel, and the film channel. The progress made by Colombian television during the first four decades of its existence is reflected in the panorama of the mid–1990s, which included three national channels (two commercial and one educational/cultural), four regional channels, and a viewership of a vast majority of the nation's population (some studies have suggested a figure as high as 98 percent of Colombia's citizenry have access to television).

The content of television programs has been a reemerging point of contention in Colombian society, and this can be explained by the subjective nature of programming decisions and the diverse political interests involved at every step. The formation of the Vigilance Committee, during the 1985 restructuring of Inravisión, was generated by the need of a "moral watchdog" to control the quality of programs; nonetheless, such an organization has not been effective due to the lack of authority to enforce its judgements. The committee, for example, rejected the series *Miami Vice* (from the United States) because of its negative portrayal of Colombia (90 percent of the drug traffickers that appeared on the program were Colombian) and its violent content. The National Council of Television agreed with the ruling, but still allowed the series to be broadcast. As early as 1955, commentaries appeared in the press expressing concerns about the effects that viewing television violence had on children: The spectacular exploits of bandidos, gangsters, and cowboys were believed to promote misguided violent tendencies in the viewers, especially children. In 1992, the opposition to these practices was such that the National Association of Advertisers (Asociación Nacional de Anunciantes—ANDA) and its affiliates published a diatribe against the programmers for using violence, brutality, sex, and drug-related themes in television programs as means of increasing viewership in order to improve ratings. One type of program that has consistently received high ratings in Colombian television is the *telenovela*.

The *telenovela*, similar to prime-time soap operas, is considered by some to be an authentically Latin American genre, which, due to its high levels of popularity, rivals North American imports.[3] The first *telenovela* to be produced and broadcast in Colombia was *In the Name of Love* (*En nombre del amor*) in 1963. Only four years later, the first awards show for *telenovelas* was aired, although the results were highly criticized by actors and actresses who regarded the judges to be largely incompetent for the task. Often denounced, like North American soap operas and other Latin American *telenovelas*, for its superficiality and questionable social value, the Colombian *telenovela* began to follow a different line of development in the 1980s, transforming it into a genre of cultural merit. Germán Rey, a Colombian professor and journalist, asserted that the *telenovela* of that time became a valuable stage for revealing the social realities of a very complex country.[4] The emergence of regional characteristics and traits facilitated the expression of cultural diversity, and current issues were integrated into the stories, making their arguments more credible. Unfortunately, according to Rey, in the late 1980s and early 1990s, the Colombian *telenovela* gradually returned to more traditional patterns, a line of development that never really ceased to exist during the genre's apogee of artistic achievement of the mid–1980s. Despite these discussions, the *telenovelas* con-

tinue to be aired with great popularity in Colombia. In the 1980s, David Sánchez Juliao's novel, *Pero sigo siendo el rey* (*But I Am Still the King*) did extremely
well adapted as a *telenovela*, and in the 1990s, the *telenovela Café* was as popular
as the World Cup or the national beauty contest.

The poor quality of television programming has often been attributed to the
commercialization of the medium in which educational and cultural interests
take a back seat to financial gain. In spite of this reality, Colombian television
has successfully been utilized as an educational tool in numerous projects. Television was first employed for educational purposes shortly after its introduction in Colombian society in rural zones where agricultural courses were
transmitted. In 1961, the International Agency for Development (Agencia Internacional para el Desarrollo—AID) launched an educational program by
television for children with the assistance of Peace Corps volunteers. The program, in some cases, reached children that had never even seen a television set
before, and it is estimated that as many as 500,000 students were exposed to
the televised instruction. There were also programs designed and implemented
for illiterate and marginalized adults in the late 1960s. In 1970, the second national channel, dedicated to educational programming, was inaugurated in the
departments of Cundinamarca, Huila, Tolima, Boyacá, and Antioquia.

The violence and terror produced by the drug cartels has not left the Colombian television industry unscathed. Jorge Enrique Pulido, a television and
radio journalist, fell victim to an assassination at the hands of drug traffickers
in 1989. A Colombian scholar, Armando Silva, has described the longest story
ever written by Colombian news programs: the case of Pablo Escobar, the
leader of the Medellín cartel.[5] Silva explains how, after the assassination of
Rodrigo Lara in 1984, the personal and public life of Escobar was illustrated on
television, almost like episodes of a *telenovela*, until his death. Silva's critique
points to the ephemeral nature of what comes across the television screen and
the effect this has on the viewer. In the case of Escobar, the episodes emphasized
sensationalism over the deep causes or inner motives underlying the actions.
The situation of drug trafficking and the broadcast media becomes more com-
plicated when individuals allegedly related to the cartels not only appear on the
evening news, but gain ownership of television companies; a recent article in
the newspaper *El Espectador* indicates that such events may have already become reality.

The future of television in Colombia depends on how current trends change
over time and the effects they have on society at large. The move towards decentralization is a key element, as well as the identity of the entities that acquire
control of the programming. The technical aspect of the future panorama will
be determined by the rate at which new advances are integrated into the Co-

lombian television system; technology such as VOD (video on demand), product sales by TV, innumerable telecommunications services, and the interactive potential of television.

RADIO

Radio is relatively important to the daily life of many Colombians, and radio communication in Colombia is among the most sophisticated in Latin America. Closely linked to the general development and growth of the nation since it was first introduced in the early 1930s, this electronic medium has been described as the communication nervous system of the nation, contributing to regional integration and thus promoting the very idea of national identity: What it means to be Colombian is understood, to a large extent, by what Colombians regularly hear about themselves on the radio.

The accomplishment of radio in Colombia should not be limited to the national boundaries, but must be understood in international terms, especially because of the field of radio journalism. One informed Colombian scholar of the media has demonstrated that Colombian radio journalism stands out worldwide for its professionalism, its technological sophistication, and the exceptional production of its human resources.[6] Nonetheless, he goes on to point out that the lack of authentic critique in the political sphere is a weakness that can be attributed to traditions of intolerance and repressive legislation.

Colombian radio has developed over several periods.[7] The first period (1929–1935) included the introduction of radio in Colombia and the experimental trials and errors that characterized its early stages, a time of rapid and chaotic growth. Similar to the adoption of television in Colombia, radio systems had already been created in several Latin American countries before the technology reached this nation. One of the first tentative steps towards the invention of the radio in a worldwide context appeared with the emergence of the wireless telegraph in 1885. This was followed by the first wireless transmission of the human voice in 1920; the first radio station was established the same year in Pittsburgh—KDKA, owned by Westinghouse. Several nations soon followed suit by acquiring the new technology and establishing radio stations, such as Denmark, Russia, Germany, Switzerland, Australia, and England. The first radio station in Latin America, and fourth in the world, was station PXW of Cuba.[8] In 1923, Colombia already had its first international station owned by Marconi Wireless Company, which controlled a world monopoly on the market. The government, under President Pedro Nel Ospina, ordered some long-wave transmitting equipment from Telefunken in 1924, but it did not arrive until 1929.

Elías Pellet Buitrago was a pioneer in Colombian radio. After studying engineering in the United States and returning to his homeland, he premiered his first radio broadcast on December 8, 1929; his station was later known as "La Voz de Barranquilla." The majority of the first stations installed were of experimental nature, both in their operation and legal status. Commercial licenses were considerably more expensive; in addition, there were only an estimated 250 radio receivers in the capital city of Bogotá in 1930, thus providing a very small audience. By 1932, this number had grown to five-thousand receivers in all of Colombia for a population of 8.4 million (compared to the twelve million receivers that had been sold in the United States). The radio *aficionados* of this period were largely technicians, many of whom had traveled abroad and come into contact with the new medium, as well as individuals who belonged to the upper economic strata. For many Colombians, the radio receivers were cost prohibitive, about eighty pesos, when an average worker earned about one peso per day, and agricultural workers even less. Nor did the radio industry provide many jobs initially; the station owners managed their broadcasting activities more like a hobby than a business, with irregular schedules and unprofessional *cuñas* (commercial slots). The people directly related to radio broadcasting were often representatives of the major manufacturing companies of radio receivers, such as Telefunken, RCA Victor, and Phillips.

Just as the history of the church in Colombia is political, so is that of radio. From the beginning, some stations had strong ties, direct or indirect, with the two traditional political parties. "Emisora HJN," for example, was under the direct control of President Enrique Olaya Herrera of the Liberal Party. In fact, Enrique Ramírez, who had previously constructed a radio transmitter from a kit, broadcast Olaya's inaugural ceremony in December of 1930. "La Voz de Colombia," founded by Jesús Amórtegui and recognized as one of the first private stations, emerged as an experiment for political broadcasting controlled by the Conservative Party. The government's use of radio extended to military operations in 1932, with the outbreak of a conflict between Colombia and Peru. Italo Amore and Roberto Jaramillo, two of the experts in radio at that time, lent their services in order to establish communications between the military forces in the field and the government leaders. These early events in the history of Colombian radio indicated the future potential of this medium to mobilize forces, whether civilian or military, and inform the people of current political and social happenings. Hernando Téllez attests to the intense regional differences of Colombia (see chapter 1), pointing out that before 1930, Colombia was a "country of countries," with a wide diversity of races, customs, traditions, and interests.[9] Radio served as a tool for national integration, helping to eliminate distances and closing the regional gaps.

Early radio programming consisted largely of music, about 80 percent of the total broadcasting time: classical, Spanish zarzuela, operetta, and popular. There was also high cultural content found in programs on literature, theater, and other areas. Practically all of the programs were live, since the technique of recording had not yet been implemented. One of the first acts of censure in Colombian radio took place in 1934, with the cancellation of "Los Josefinos," broadcast by the station HJN, for the alleged immorality of the program.

The second period of development (1935–1948) in Colombian radio was characterized by the rapid growth and commercialization of the medium, as well as the first attempts at forming radio networks. In general, the economic climate of Colombia improved during this period: There was a substantial increase in coffee exports, manufacturing factories were constructed, primary resources were imported, and national markets were fortified. Many industries began to see the radio as an effective medium for advertising, and thus invested in commercial slots, which in turn led to organizational restructuring in many stations; a business approach to management was implemented on the previously haphazard arrangements. Much of this reform can be attributed to the Revolución en Marcha (initiated by Alfonso López Pumarejo), a fundamental part of the Liberal project aimed at the modernization of Colombia. The statistics effectively illustrate the rapid growth in the radio industry: In 1934, there were seventeen registered stations; in 1939, forty-four stations; and by 1941, seventy stations. Three of the principal stations in Bogotá at that time were: "Emisora Nueva Granada," "La Voz de la Víctor," and "La Voz de Colombia."

With the rapid growth of this period, some of the precursors to the future dominant radio networks of Colombia emerged. In 1937, the program *La Alfombra Mágica* (The Magic Carpet), created by Enrique Ramírez Gaviria, was transmitted daily by six different radio stations. The German company Bayer introduced the network "Cadena Azul Bayer" into the Colombian radio system in 1940, and its programs were broadcast by approximately twenty stations. Another foreign network entered the competition simultaneously, "Cadena Kresto" of Argentina. The success of these two foreign enterprises resulted in the formation of a Colombian network, "Cadena Bolívar" (1941), established by Jaime García and Hernando Téllez. The initial success of these three networks dissipated with the arrival of World War II, although they definitely marked the way for future, long-lasting trends. Shortwave broadcasting still dominated this era, and the primary competitive battles between stations took place in the form of increases in the power of transmitters.

The aforementioned expansion in the radio industry was accompanied by innovations in the programming sparked by the desire to increase the number of listeners, promoting the products advertised. The station "La Voz de Antioquia" made history for its spectacular live shows, and also taking the stage were some of the first Colombian comedies, the character of "Jorgito," created by Raúl Echeverri, being among the more popular. With respect to music, the program "Novedad" (1935) popularized the bolero (see chapter 8). The melo-dramatic *radionovela* (a genre that might be described as a radio soap opera) is a probable predecessor of the *telenovela*; *Yon-Fu* (1938) is credited with being one of the first of these programs to captivate audiences. This genre initially emerged in the United States during the Great Depression of the 1930s; it pro-vided its listeners with romance, intrigue, and suspense—effective distractions from the hunger, unemployment, and social tension that predominated dur-ing that period. In the early 1940s, another adaptation from the radio industry of the United States appeared: *programas de concursos* (game shows). One of the most noteworthy and popular of these numerous game shows was *Coltejar Toca a su Puerta* (Coltejar Knocks on Your Door), in which a specially deco-rated car raced through the city, randomly stopping upon receiving orders from the station, and the driver knocked on the door of the nearest house. If the residents were listening to that radio station, they received a prize. With the advent of television in the 1950s, the radio game shows eventually diminished.

A tragic event in 1935 led to the initiation of Colombian radio journalism. Heretofore, the *radioperiódicos* (radio newscasts) basically consisted of the broadcasting of brief news events (often read directly from newspapers) and political or cultural speeches. It appears that the political inclinations assumed by the producers of the *radioperiódicos* were predicated by the party with which they were associated. As a case in point, the first *radioperiódico*, "La República Liberal" transmitted by the station "La Voz de la Víctor," was established by López Pumarejo during his presidency. The conservatives soon thereafter founded their own radio station, "La Voz de Colombia" (1936), in addition to purchasing the newspaper *El Siglo*. These radio newscasts were a volatile type of program due to the potentially political implications of their content. None-theless, they proliferated throughout Colombia during this time period, pri-marily due to the fact that the democratic governments in power were hesitant to limit the freedom of expression in the media. The potential of the *radio-periódicos* drastically changed in June of 1935, when Antonio Henao Gaviria, a young journalist, went to the Olaya Herrera Airport in Medellín upon receiv-ing notice of a tragic accident in which the internationally known singer Carlos Gardel was killed. Henao Gaviria communicated the details of the tragedy by telephone to Gustavo Rodas Isaza of "La Voz de Antioquia," who in turn trans-mitted the news on live radio to his listeners. This event changed the nature of Colombian radio newscasts, increasing the instantaneity of breaking news and suggesting other political uses for this medium. (Today, Colombian radio is extremely effective in broadcasting news "as it is happening.")

The desire to protect the freedom of expression did not always predominate the legislation that governed Colombian radio. In fact, a law was proposed in 1936 which sought to nationalize the medium. Members of the press, fearful of government control over any medium of communication, allied themselves with the radio stations, and eventually the project was rejected, although a less severe law was passed. In the same year, the creation of station names that were directly related to commercial products or that included foreign words was prohibited; another law forbade the broadcasting of news items of political character. These restraints placed on radio can be attributed in part to the chaotic situation that had arisen around this medium since its inception and had caused many serious problems in the industry: the proliferation of stations, the overabundance of *radioperiódicos*, the aggressively belligerent politics in the capital, and the poor quality of the facilities.

The ability of radio to instantaneously reach the public with transmissions converted it, at times, into an instrument for mobilizing the masses, usually in actions against the government in power, but sometimes to maintain power. In 1937, a decentralist movement emerged in opposition to some of the policies proposed by President Alfonso López Pumarejo. The radio stations of Medellín, headed by "La Voz de Antioquia" and supporting the regionalist interest groups, utilized their transmissions to mobilize the people for a massive demonstration protesting the propositions. On another noteworthy occasion, the radio was seized and completely controlled by the government in order to reassure and calm the public during a military coup; this took place in 1944, when President López Pumarejo was taken prisoner by Colonel Heriberto Gil. The government minister Lleras Camargo informed the public over the airwaves that the majority of the military forces supported the president and the situation was stable—Gil eventually surrendered. Only four years later, an incident known as the *Bogotazo* occurred.

The *Bogotazo* can symbolically be seen as the beginning of the third period (1948–1960) in the history of Colombian radio since it generated numerous drastic changes, not only in the radio industry, but in the nation as a whole. It has been described how the period known as La Violencia was sparked by the assassination of one of the leaders of the Liberal Party, Jorge Eliécer Gaitán, on April 9, 1948 (see chapter 1). This event also had multiple repercussions in the radio industry, especially in the immediate aftermath of the assassination. The news of this crime was first broadcast on the program *Ultimas Noticias*, and shortly thereafter a group led by the journalists of two newspapers, *El Liberal* and *La Razón y El Tiempo*, seized control of the station "La Nueva Granada" and forced the radio announcers to continue transmitting *Ultimas Noticias*. Left-wing politicians attempted to take advantage of the situation and channel the public outrage into a revolution. The station "Radiodifusora Nacional" was also taken over by left-wing activists, composed of a group of university students headed by the poet Jorge Zalamea Borda and the army captain Phillips, who subsequently transmitted misleading news proclaiming the success of revolutionary actions. Although similar uprisings and conflicts surfaced in Cali, Puerto Tejada, Huila, Tolima, and other areas, these transmissions only served to heighten the rioting and violence in the streets, and the government soon retook the radio stations.

The consequences of radio participation in the *Bogotazo*, whether willing or coerced, and yet again the frightening demonstration of radio's power to mobilize the masses led to drastic intervention by the government. This took shape primarily in the establishment of the National Association of Radio Broadcasting (Asociación Nacional de Radiodifusión—ANRADIO), which immediately suspended all radio licenses and thus acquired an indisputable control over the medium that the government had never before possessed. This tight rein over radio continued into the 1950s, and the industry was characterized by control, censure, and repression during the presidency of Laureano Gómez and the military regime of Rojas Pinilla.

The self-censorship of many stations reduced their political commentary, whether direct or indirect, to complete neutrality. The *radionovela*, which constituted approximately 40 percent of the programming of this period, closely adhered to the self-censorship policy by emphasizing an individualized world in which social, economic, and political conditions were irrelevant. Live musical programs, in spite of their previous popularity, all but disappeared in this period due to the introduction of phonographic technology and the role played by disc jockeys—and, of course, the launching of rock 'n' roll was fundamental. Sports programs were a considerably important part of the radio broadcast, providing about 25 percent of the total programming. Also, Bogotá's first "Radio Reloj" (twenty-four-hours-a-day news program) appeared in 1952.

Although the radio programming during this period was greatly driven by commercial tendencies and the need to increase ratings, some efforts were made to improve the cultural content on the airwaves. "HJCK—El Mundo de Bogotá" is one remarkable example of a cultural station that has not only managed to withstand competitive pressures from the huge networks for more than four decades, but also has achieved internationally distinguished programming. Inaugurated in 1950 by Alvaro Castaño Castillo and Eduardo Caballero Calderón, HJCK, commonly known as the "station of the intellectuals," was the first Latin American station to receive the Spanish "ONDAS" Award for cultural broadcasting. Another notable station created without profit motives was "Radio Sutatenza," an innovative experiment conceived in 1949 by the priest José Joaquín Salcedo to transmit programs aimed at teaching basic literacy to rural workers (see chapter 2). The broadcasts were complemented by instructors in the audience with the listeners who provided follow-up explanations and written materials. The project stimulated international interest, and UNESCO supplied technical and cultural assistance at one time, although eventually Monsignor José Joaquín Salcedo sought the commercialization of the station.

The commercialization and expansion of Colombian radio, dominated by the major networks, proceeded forward in spite of the tightened governmental controls. Founded in 1948 upon the merger of three stations: "Emisoras Nuevo Mundo," "La Voz de Antioquia," and "RCO," the "Cadena Radial Colombiana" (CARACOL) was one of the first networks to be established. Only one year later, in 1949, the second major network, RCN ("Radio Cadena Nacional"), came into existence, controlling the combined broadcasting potential of "Nueva Granada" and "Radio Medellín." The third powerhouse to enter the network arena appeared initially in 1953 as the station "La Voz de Cali," but later became known as "Circuito TODELAR" (1956), TODELAR being an acronym formed from the founder's surname, Tobón de la Roche. These three networks were created and developed within an intricate system of industrial financing, political alliances, and intense market competition, and the primary battlefields were found in some of the major Colombian cities: Cali, Medellín, Barranquilla, and Bogotá.

An important technological advance that can be seen as an opening for the fourth period in the history of radio (1960 to the present) was the appearance of the transistor radio at the end of the 1950s. The transistor was the catalyst for the expansion of radio broadcasting to the massive dimensions that characterize it in current times. The statistics illustrate this point: In 1952, there were approximately 500,000 radio receivers in Colombia; in 1959, 2,084,287 receivers; in 1964, 5,250,000; and in 1972, 12,000,000. The transistor radio was more accessible to the populace, and more importantly, it granted the listener more freedom and mobility because it operated on batteries. Reynaldo Pareja also points out some important factors that stimulated the increase in the number of radio receivers in the nation: the popularity of soccer, the visit from the pope in 1968, and the moon expedition of the United States in 1969.[10] In order to experience these events more directly, people obtained radios. Nonetheless, radio was not to monopolize the airwaves in the future, as the world of media became increasingly more complex starting in 1954.

The consolidation of the major radio networks in the 1950s coincided with the emergence of television in Colombian society; this new medium was seen as another competitor for the desired commercial financing, but also as a fertile field to be exploited by radio leaders. The three principal radio networks, CARACOL, RCN, and TODELAR, all of which already had links with the print media, soon established ties in the television system. In spite of the fact that a considerable percentage of the commercial advertisers switched to television to promote their products, the radio networks continued growing and acquiring more member stations. Counting the stations owned by the networks or affiliated with them, by 1975 CARACOL had sixty-six stations, RCN had fifty-four, and TODELAR had seventy. The advertising industry should also be mentioned in this context since it has propelled the expansion of the media to a great degree and has always been a point of contention with respect to the financing and content of what is printed or broadcast. In the mid–1970s, advertising had already become one of the three largest industries in Colombia. It has become an important element in the Colombian economy, especially when one considers that in 1977 the same amount of money was spent on advertising as that budgeted by the government for the expansion of the educational system.

One Colombian scholar explains the history of Colombian radio by building an argument against the system on which it was modeled since its very inception: the radio industry of the United States. According to this scholar, the radio (in addition to the other media) serves as an instrument in the economic, technical, and cultural neocolonialism imposed on Colombia, which is sustained by a dependency on the United States. At the same time, he acknowledges the important role that radio has played in the development of the nation and the regional integration and communication that it has facilitated, transforming this "country of countries" into a more unified nation.

NEWSPAPERS

The Colombian press, often referred to in Colombia as *la gran prensa* (the great press), has commonly been known as the most prestigious and credible of the mass media in Colombia. Numerous prominent figures in Colombian society have been involved in the newspaper industry, from presidents to authors. In fact, before becoming an internationally famous novelist, Gabriel García Márquez worked as a journalist (see chapter 7). He was studying at the National University in Bogotá when Jorge Eliécer Gaitán was assassinated in 1948; because of the turmoil of the *Bogotazo* the university was temporarily closed, and García Márquez traveled to Cartagena where he began working for the newspaper *El Universal* at the age of twenty. Since then, he has collaborated and written for numerous other newspapers. A predisposition toward the press as a source of credible information, especially with respect to political issues, can be largely attributed to the very high prestige of literacy and the written word; as a case in point, a study of a Colombian village in the 1960s showed that 59 percent of the people purchased a newspaper, although only 58 percent were literate.

The first Colombian publication recognized as a newspaper appeared at the end of the eighteenth century, more than three hundred years after the invention of the printing press in Europe. This three-century delay in the arrival of this technological advance in Colombia can be traced back to Spain. The German Johannes Gensfleisch von Gutenberg invented the printing press in 1440, and in 1474 it arrived in Spain, then under the rule of the Catholic monarchs Ferdinand and Isabella. During the sixteenth century, the Catholic Counter Reformation and the Inquisition led to stringent controls of the press and the censorship of many publications, and in 1524, the *Consejo de Indias* was established as the most powerful legislative body in Latin America; the *Consejo* took part in the regulation of the press. *Nueva España*, the region presently called Mexico, was the first in Latin America to receive a printing press in 1533, and the technology gradually extended and reached the following areas: Peru (1581), Guatemala (1660), Paraguay (1680), Argentina (1705), and La Habana (1707).[11] The Jesuits brought the first printing press to Colombia in 1737, and Brother Francisco de la Peña, originally from Madrid, began publishing novenas, books on doctrine, and other religious materials. In 1741, the Spanish Crown refused to issue a printing permit to the Jesuit priests, but they continued printing religious materials until 1767, when they were expelled. By taking these initial steps, nevertheless, the Jesuits contributed significantly to the development of the press in Colombia.

The first newspaper in Latin America (similar, at least, to what is considered a newspaper in modern times) was the *Gazeta de México*, which first appeared in 1722. In Colombia, some journalistic precursors appeared in July of 1785 after an earthquake shook the capital city; the authors of this early publication are unknown, but it is assumed that an order of friar monks printed and distributed the four-page *Aviso del Terremoto*, which described the event giving details of the injuries and damages caused by the tremor. Two follow-ups were printed with more details, and then in August of the same year, the *Gazeta de Santa Fe de Bogotá Capital del Nuevo Reyno de Granada* was created, but only rendered three numbers before disappearing. The first true newspaper of Colombia was initiated by a Cuban immigrant, Manuel del Socorro Rodríguez, who, with the economic support of the viceroy, printed the *Papel Periódico de la*

Ciudad de Sante Fe de Bogotá in 1791. This newspaper lasted approximately six years and reached over more than four-hundred subscribers, which at that time was a considerable number. Four years later in 1801, the weekly *Correo Curioso* appeared, produced by José Luis de Azuola y Lozano and Jorge Tadeo Lozano. This newspaper was not as fortunate as its predecessor and survived less than a year with only forty subscribers. Jorge Tadeo Lozano later became the president of Cundinamarca in 1811, but was forced to resign and eventually was sentenced to death for treason. A few other early newspapers can be included in this preliminary stage of the Colombian press: *El Redactor Americano* (1806), *El Alternativo del Radactor Americano* (1807), and *Semanario del Nuevo Reyno de Granada* (1808).

These early newspapers were, in essence, of colonial nature; they were edited by the Royal Press and produced in the context of an elitist class composed of Spaniards or their descendants. The content of the weeklies was focused on the interests of this elite: literature, science, economics, moral philosophy, matters of official character. The brief existence of most of these publications can be attributed to the difficulties of financing, which, without the assistance of the state, promised their demise; the paper was expensive, and there were few subscribers.

Gustavo Otero Muñoz affirms that true Colombian journalism began with the publication of *Diario Político de Santafé de Bogotá*, founded by Francisco José de Caldas and Joaquín Camacho in 1810, whereas the previous newspapers were basically collections of essays.[12] The *Diario* was of political nature, serving as the medium for the first calls for independence and freedom—it was revolutionary journalism. With this, the journalism of opposition appeared; among the supporters of colonial independence surfaced polemical differences with regard to constitutional questions, the balance of leadership, and other issues. Much of this dissent was expressed in the publications of the early nineteenth century, such as *El Argos Americano*, *El Argos al Público*, *La Constitución Feliz*, and *La Bagatela*.

The story behind the founder of *La Bagatela* is significant to the history of Colombia as a nation and the development of the press. In December of 1793, Antonio Amador José Nariño Alvarez of Bogotá secretly published *Derechos del Hombre y del Ciudadano*, a document based on a translation of a book about the French Revolution of 1789. Shortly thereafter, Nariño was denounced for the publication of the seditious document and sentenced to ten years of incarceration in an African prison. While being held in Spain, he escaped and proceeded to live in Great Britain, France, Venezuela, and finally managed to return to his homeland, only to be incarcerated again. Eventually in 1810, Nariño was released by the new government, and soon returned to his previous journalistic endeavors, reprinting the *Derechos del Hombre* and, in 1811, launching *La Bagatela*.[13] Although his writing was often characterized as having a cynical and mocking tone, Nariño consistently demanded liberty and freedom in the pages of his newspaper, an aspect that makes *La Bagatela* exemplify this period of revolutionary change.

From the first declaration of independence in 1810, until the formation of the Regeneration, innumerable newspapers emerged only to disappear shortly afterwards, much of this due to the political and economic instability of the period. The freedom of the press and the character of the newspaper depended on the ruling party, and the subsequent shifts of power, civil wars, and constitutional changes all had their effect on the print medium. As illustrated by the examples of Jorge Tadeo Lozano and Antonio Nariño, the press was a popular instrument for expounding political viewpoints. *El Correo del Orinoco* (1818) was published under the orders of Simón Bolívar, well aware of the potential of the print media, as a herald of the final triumph of the revolution. Many of the publications that appeared during this immediate post-revolution era of La Gran Colombia served primarily as stages from which the rivaling factions polemicized current issues—newspapers such as *El Patriota, Los Toros de Fucha, El Insurgente, La Indicación*, and *Gaceta de Colombia*.[14] Also during this period, the first Colombian bilingual newspaper appeared, *El Constitucional*, published in a Spanish-English double edition.

After the separation of Venezuela and Ecuador and the founding of the República de Nueva Granada in 1831, the political press basically followed two lines of development: the official line, inspired by the government; and the popular line, inspired by the opposition. Some of the newspapers that stood out during this period include: *La Gaceta de Colombia, El Granadino, El Cultivador Cundinamarquez*, and *El Cacheco de Bogotá*. Julio Arboleda is praised as a noteworthy Colombian journalist of this period, well known for his measured writing style. After spending more than seven years in England, France, and Italy, Arboleda returned to his homeland in 1838 and collaborated in several newspapers, including *El Republicano, El Independiente, El Patriota, El Payanés, El Siglo*, and *El Misóforo*. After the civil war of 1840, the conservatives and the liberals solidified their identities, and the press became even more partisan than before, clearly marking the diametrically opposed ideas of the respective parties. *El Progreso, El Nacional, La América, El Aviso*, and *El Conservador* are some of the newspapers of this era. In contrast to the aforementioned newspapers, predominantly of political orientation, Otero Muñoz notes that many literary, satirical, and humorous publications emerged in the nineteenth century.

Founded in January of 1855 and still in existence today, *El Tiempo* is generally considered the most important newspaper in Colombia. Under the direction of José María Samper, *El Tiempo* was designed following the model of the major European newspapers of that time; its format went beyond political radicalism and included literary and cultural information. Since its birth, *El Tiempo* has ceased operation several times, and was out of circulation at the end of the nineteenth century, then reemerged in 1911 under the ownership and direction of Eduardo Santos, one of several journalists to occupy the presidency of Colombia. To compete with *El Tiempo*, José Ortiz founded *El Porvenir*, a newspaper with conservative inclinations, but equal in dimensions and format to its rival.

The two decades prior to the Regeneration, from 1861 to 1880, the Liberal Party remained politically weak, and the publications, therefore, generally were limited to content favorable to the party in power. A handful of the newspapers that belong to this era are *La Gazeta de Santander*, *El Mercurio*, *El Monitor*, *El Nuevo Mundo*, *La Tribuna*, and *El Deber*. Also noteworthy, in 1878 the first publication directed by a woman, Soledad Acosta de Samper, appeared: *La Mujer*, which was composed of articles written with Colombian females as the intended readers.

Although the Regeneration was characterized by a consolidating transformation of Colombian politics, Gabriel Fonnegra refers to this period as a return to the Middle Ages with respect to the governmental control of the press.[15] The notorious Law 61, denoted *la ley de los caballos* (the law of the horses) by Fidel Cano and enacted in 1888, granted an absolute power to the government to administratively repress those crimes that disrupted the public order; in effect, a number of newspapers were suspended and journalists were incarcerated or exiled, supposedly because of the abuses committed in their profession. This restraint of the press was extreme, and according to Fonnegra, "to write about Rafael Núñez or Miguel Antonio Caro was a mortal risk."[16] In spite of this repressive environment, a myriad of publications surfaced in the late nineteenth century; the majority were short-lived, but some were longer lasting: *Las Noticias*, *El Taller*, *El Telegrama*, and *El Heraldo*. *El Correo Nacional*, established in 1890 by Carlos Martínez Silva, initiated the practice of publishing interviews and paying reporters for this work, thus creating a more distinguishable profession for these writers. As one of the first stable publications, this newspaper marked a new era in Colombian journalism and was avidly read by its subscribers. Another enduring publication was *El Espectador*, which is presently a major Colombian newspaper, although it was closed by the government of the Regeneration. Fidel Cano, well known for his tenacious pursuit of the freedom of the press, founded this newspaper in 1887, a time in which there were no liberal newspapers in circulation.

The Colombian press of the early twentieth century was characterized by an increase in the number of newspapers, but generally they were ephemeral "mini-newspapers" of less than ten pages with very limited distribution; most had a small circle of local readers, and the major newspapers of the capital did not achieve consistent national circulation until the 1930s. The predominance of regionalistic tendencies during most of the nineteenth century and the early twentieth century was reflected in the development of the press, largely hindering the creation of a more nationally integrated print medium. Although commercial advertisements were gradually becoming an important source of financing, these newspapers were still largely supported by the public, which helps to explain why between 1900 and 1934 more than a hundred different titles of diverse publications fleetingly appeared and disappeared.

Since the midtwentieth century, the Colombian press has suffered periods of censure and, in some cases, outright attacks. During the *Bogotazo*, at least ten newspapers (primarily of conservative tendencies) were destroyed throughout Colombia, and during La Violencia, both liberal and conservative newspapers were closed, burned, and pillaged. Rojas Pinilla initially mitigated the oppression, but soon thereafter closed, censured, and fined various newspapers. In more recent times, confrontations with drug traffickers has led to the bombing of newspaper offices and the injury or death of journalists, such as Guillermo Cano, the editor of *El Espectador* who was slain in an ambush in 1986. The 1989 crackdown on the cartel caused repercussions in the press as the drug traffickers took their vengeance on the more outspoken opposing papers. Many Colombian journalists have been forced into *autocensura* (self-censorship) as a question of survival.

In contrast to the defensive posture caused by violence against the press, investigative journalism has been integrated into Colombian newspaper coverage. Just as the work of North American journalists Carl Bernstein and Bob Woodward on Watergate in 1972 led to the emergence of investigative reporting in the United States, a similar type of journalism has been popular in Colombia since the 1980s. Daniel Samper is one journalist known for his work of this type, and investigative teams have been formed by several newspapers, including *El Espectador*, *Vanguardia Liberal*, and *El Heraldo*.

In the late 1970s, there were forty-two daily newspapers in sixteen Colombian cities, two of which, *El Espectador* and *El Tiempo* of Bogotá, each had a circulation of 200,000. The primary newspaper of Medellín, *El Colombiano*, claimed a daily circulation of 100,000. Other important newspapers of this period included *El Espacio* (Bogotá), *El Heraldo* (Barranquilla), *La Vanguardia* (Bucaramanga), *El País* (Cali), *Occidente* (Cali), *El Siglo* (Bogotá), and *La República* (Bogotá). The investment of advertising companies has been an essential stimulus to the growth of the newspaper industry, without which the rapid expansion would have been practically impossible. In 1983, commercial advertising provided 85 percent of the income of *El Tiempo*, and only 15 percent was generated by newspaper sales. In addition, the majority of the actual space within the newspaper was allotted to advertising, about 64 percent, whereas news, commentary, and other information composed the remainder. Another more recent trend in the newspaper medium has been the establishment of ties with and in some cases ownership by large financial groups. Practically since its inception, the press has been allied to political parties, but by placing the control of a medium of communication in the hands of capital-driven entities, even more dangerous implications are on the horizon for the credibility of information printed and the freedom of press in the future.

Given the ongoing political crises and exceptional violence in Colombia in recent years, the media (press, radio, and television) have had a central role to play in daily life. Radio is the medium that has informed most Colombians most immediately as the almost daily crises have evolved. The current state of the media is a complex, interconnected structure, inviting a thorough examination of the ties and alliances among innumerable entities. These include the two traditional political parties, advertising companies, financial groups, members of the social and political upper echelon, among others, in addition to the powerful influences of foreign countries. The future of the media will be based on the interaction of these complex structures with the advancing technological breakthroughs, as well as the role that governmental intervention may play.

5

The Performing Arts: Cinema, Theater, and Music

The Colombian film industry dates back to the early part of the twentieth century; while music and theater have roots that go back several centuries to the colonial period. None of the three, however, enjoys either the tradition or production equivalent to nations such as Brazil, Mexico, and Argentina. Rather, they should be understood within the context of a variety of factors that have shaped society and culture in modern Colombia, forces such as: the political conflict of the 1950s, known as La Violencia; the movement of literary rebels in the 1960s, known as *Nadaísmo*; and the presence of Gabriel García Márquez, among other factors. In the 1960s and 1970s, when Colombian film was first consolidating into what some were calling the *nuevo cine colombiano* (new Colombian film), Colombian film directors were strongly influenced by the new Cuban film movement of the 1960s and what was called *Cinema Novo* in Brazil.

Music has been strongly affected by Colombia's Caribbean culture, and theater by one of the major figures of the twentieth century in Latin America, Enrique Buenaventura. Along with the international recognition of the excellence of Buenaventura's theater, the recent parallel in music would be the awarding of a Grammy in the United States to two *boleros* composed by Fabio Salgado Mejía ("Estéfano") and sung by the Cuban American pop star Gloria Estefan. In terms of international recognition and commercial success, Colombian music has been, by far, the most outstanding of the three performing arts. Two major figures in Colombian music today are mezzo-soprano Martha Senn and Caribbean singer Carlos Vives, whose international success in the

1990s is yet another indicator of the preeminence of Colombian popular music in Latin America.

The performance of theater and music in Colombia had a historical turning point in 1793, with the construction of the theater Coliseo Ramírez. The Spanish entrepreneur José Tomás Ramírez built the Coliseo Ramírez in conjunction with José Dionisio de Villar, and they inaugurated the building for an audience of two hundred—which was for a traveling company from Spain that featured the Spanish singer and dancer Nicolasa Villar. Eventually changing its name to Teatro Maldonado, this theater was the setting for the most important ongoing performing arts in Colombia in the nineteenth century. During this period, Colombians attended opera (usually seeing European traveling companies) with great enthusiasm and even fury. By late in the century, the theater building had deteriorated physically, and was replaced by the present-day Teatro Colón, which opened in 1892 with the showing of an opera.

Generally speaking, theater and film always struggle for survival in Colombia, where economic resources are relatively limited and the public sparse. Music, on the other hand, is a thriving international industry in Colombia.

COLOMBIAN FILM

Film in Colombia began with the silent films imported and distributed by an Italian family, the Di Domenicos, and has culminated with the presence of a relatively small but vital film industry in the 1980s and 1990s. Four brothers and cousins of the Di Domenico family brought European films to Colombia in the latter part of the first decade of the twentieth century. In 1908 and 1909, they showed films in Bogotá and Medellín, and by the second decade, movie houses had sprung up across Colombia's major cities, as well as in some small towns, such as Sincelejo. In some regions of warm and tropical climate, the films were shown in outdoor theaters. Some of the famed movie theaters of this pioneer period in Colombian film were the Teatro Olympia in Bogotá, the Teatro Gallera in Medellín, and the Salón Sincelejo in Sincelejo.

The Di Domenico brothers remained the catalyzing force for the exhibition of movies in Colombia for two decades. They were responsible for importing, distributing, and showing most of the films seen in Colombia until 1918, when the distribution and showing of films were disassociated for the first time. Nevertheless, the Di Domenicos continued as the principal importers and distributors of films in Colombia until 1927, the year Cine Colombia was founded, and the Di Domenicos retired from business.

In these pioneer days, film was well received in Colombia, although its presence was anomalous in such a traditional society that in many ways still lived life—particularly in the provinces—as if it were still in the nineteenth century. Writers have observed this unusual situation, from turn-of-the-century realist Tomás Carrasquilla to García Márquez. Carrasquilla published an essay in 1914 pointing out how film, unlike (realist) literature lent itself to the marvelous and magical. In a hilarious anecdote in García Márquez's *One Hundred Years of Solitude*, a movie is shown in a small-town theater in which actors appear who had died in a previous film. The outraged customers, who feel deceived, throw their chairs at the screen, creating a riot in the movie house.

Colombian filmgoers were as interested in the new possibilities of sound with movies as were their counterparts in the United States and Europe. In 1925, in fact, when an airplane departed in the movie *Bajo el cielo antioqueño,* an enterprising movie house owner started a car engine outside—at the exact same time for the necessary sound effects. It was not until 1929, however (two years after *The Jazz Singer* in the United States), that Carlos E. Schroeder began producing the first Colombian films with sound ("talkies") and was joined soon thereafter by Luis David Peña.

The Colombian film industry has always been of relatively small proportions, but a few struggling companies arose in the 1930s and 1940s that produced films. Colombia Films was established in 1938, and played a major role in making movies. The leaders of Colombian film during this period were Directors Luis David Peña and Máximo Calvo. The Colombian movie star of the 1940s was the actress Lily Alvarez, who appeared in numerous films. The movies of this period, such as Máximo Calvo's *Flores del Valle* (1941), tended to emphasize the folkloric, as well as regional customs. Much film production consisted of short documentary works that either recounted social life (*crónica social*) or made political announcements.

In the 1950s, a small number of film directors made an effort to move Colombian film beyond the confines of the folkloric themes that had dominated in both film and literature, to a large degree, under the influence of the classic novel *La vorágine* (*The Vortez,* 1924) and similar *criollista* works of the 1930s and 1940s. These *criollista* novelists and film directors sought to establish Colombian identity by exalting national values. Typically, they found a special relationship between the new national identity and the new land of the Americas. Consequently, the novels produced by *criollistas* are sometimes called "novels of the land." On one hand, some films began to present the *campesino* in contexts other than the folkloric, such as in a setting of political violence—the civil war of La Violencia. On the other hand, the novelist Alvaro Cepeda Samudio launched a more avant-garde project, creating the film *La langosta azul* (1954). This innovative film—the first of its type in Colombia—had no plot and made no attempt at the mimetic description of Colombian reality.

Cepeda Samudio belonged to a group of young intellectuals in Barranquilla who, in the late 1940s and early 1950s, held great hope for modernizing Colombian culture. They read William Faulkner and the other modernist writers from the United States and Europe, and they were just as fascinated with contemporary film. In addition to Cepeda Samudio, this "Group of Barranquilla" (as it was designated years later) included García Márquez, Germán Vargas, Alfonso Fuenmayor, and Alejandro Obregón (see chapters 6, 7, and 8).

García Márquez, unlike his friend Alvaro Cepeda Samudio, did not attempt to make any films in the 1950s, but he did contribute to the Colombian film process with the movie reviews he published in newspapers. In the late 1940s and early 1950s, he wrote a daily column for the newspaper *El Heraldo* in Barranquilla, which included occasional film reviews or brief commentary on movies he had seen. Later, in 1954–1955, he wrote film reviews more systematically for *El Espectador* in Bogotá. García Márquez was so interested in film, in fact, that in the early 1960s he moved to Mexico with the intention of abandoning his writing career and directing all his efforts toward film. He worked on several film scripts in that period (including a project with the Mexican writer Carlos Fuentes) before eventually turning to the writing of *One Hundred Years of Solitude.*

In the 1950s, Colombian film began finding firmer ground on which to consolidate and flourish, enough for some critics to speak not only of a *nuevo cine colombiano* (*new Colombian film*), but even of a "boom" of Colombian film. Alvaro Cepeda Samudio continued working in film until his death in 1972, directing the short documentaries *Noticiero del Caribe* (1968), *Carnaval en el Caribe* (1969), and *La subienda* (1972). Santiago García, who later became prominent in Colombia for his work in theater, directed the film *Bajo la tierra* in the 1960s. Ciro Durán, Alberto Giraldo Castro, Francisco Norden, and Jorge Pinto began directing films in the 1960s, and remained active enough to become recognized film directors by the 1970s.

A turning point for modern film in Colombia was 1967, the year two groundbreaking films appeared. The first was José María Arzuaga's *Pasado al meridiano,* which had a story line dealing with Colombian identity. It offered new, experimental aesthetics for filmmaking in Colombia—carried out with a minimal budget, handheld cameras, and work over a three- to four-month period. This "aesthetics of poverty" (as the producers called it), nevertheless, produced a novel film of the moment. The other groundbreaking film of 1967 was *Camilo Torres,* directed by Diego León Giraldo, a documentary work dealing with the life of the revolutionary priest Camilo Torres. It effectively denounced the government forces in opposition to Camilo Torres, thus assuming a position of political commitment rarely seen in Colombian film before 1967.

Colombian filmmakers became professionalized in the 1970s in a way that had never before been possible in Colombia. A major reason for this transformation was the passage of a law in 1971 that provided for taxing commercial film exhibitors, channeling funds into the production of Colombian short films that were required to be shown before all commerical movies. As a result of this new support, Colombian documentary work flourished, and thus was able to experiment with numerous themes and techniques new to Colombian film.

A major film to appear in Colombia in the early 1970s was *Chircales* (1972), by Jorge Silva and Marta Rodríguez, a documentary work that the two film directors dedicated five years to developing. Set in the working-class and impoverished south side of Bogotá, *Chircales* is a forty-two-minute film in 16 mm, dealing with an impoverished family working in subhuman conditions in a brick factory. Seen primarily through the eyes of a young child in the family, it is a technical accomplishment that set new standards for Colombian documentary film.

Under the influence of the new Cuban film and *Cinema Novo* from Brazil, other Colombian filmmakers found a new voice in the early 1970s, continuing the political work of their 1960s predecessors. This film was identified in Colombia as *tercer cine* (third film), *cine marginal* (marginal film), *cine militante* (militant film), or *cine independiente* (independent film). In addition to Jorge Silva and Marta Rodríguez, the practitioners of this new film included Carlos Alvarez, Carlos Mayolo, and Luis Ospina.

Since the 1970s, Colombian filmmakers and critics have engaged in lengthy debates over the status of Colombian film in a nation overwhelmed by American productions from Hollywood. They have also discussed the conditions necessary for producing films that might compete for an international audience. Despite the ongoing "crisis" of the Colombian filmmaking industry, the 1980s and 1990s have witnessed the production of several noteworthy films. Francisco Norden's *Cóndores no entierran todos los días* (1984) is an excellent adaption of the novel by Gustavo Alvarez Gardeazábal of the same title. It relates the story of the political violence of La Violencia, revealing some of the horrors of the period that had not been in the public forum before Alvarez Gardeazábal and Norden produced their respective works. The setting is the town of Tuluá in the Valle del Cauca, where La Violencia had been particularly intense in the late 1940s and 1950s.

Lisandro Duque and Sergio Cabrera have also created major contributions to contemporary Colombian film. Cabrera's *La estrategia del caracol* is considered one of Colombia's better contemporary films. It deals with a group of urban residents whom the government attempts to evict from their homes. The film shows the unique response of these resistant urban dwellers, their "strategy" for survival.

More recently, Víctor Gaviria directed *La vendedora de rosas,* which was quite successful in the Cannes Film Festival in 1998. Gaviria works in the streets of Medellín with a testimonial film that demonstrates his commitment to social change in Colombia. Urban Medellín has been a focus of crime and social disorder in Colombia since the late 1980s.

García Márquez and a few other Colombian writers have continued their interest in film and have continued to make contributions to its development in Colombia and Latin America. In the 1980s, García Márquez frequently traveled to Cuba to offer free film workshops to young Cubans, teaching the art of writing film scripts and other basics of film. In the 1990s, he helped to organize and promote an annual international film festival in Cartagena. This film festival always attracts a few star directors and actors from the United States, Europe, and Latin America, thus providing indirect support for the Colombian film industry.

Two Colombian writers have been involved with film criticism, a genre that has been virtually nonexistent in Colombia. In the mid–1970s, the young writer Andrés Caicedo published *Ojo al cine*, a sophisticated magazine of film critique. Caicedo's premature death ended this unique project for a special and much-needed organ in Colombia. The postmodern novelist Alberto Duque López has dedicated a lifetime to film criticism, writing film reviews and publishing interviews with film directors and actors during the last three decades of the twentieth century. Duque López's reviews and publications on Latin American, European, and American film are the work of an expert; he has done much to educate Colombians about both the best and the worst of the movies available for viewing in Colombia.

The Colombian film industry is struggling as much today as it was in the 1960s and 1970s. An occasional outstanding Colombian film by the likes of Sergio Cabrera or Lisandro Duque can draw an interested Colombian public, even though the vast majority of films seen in Colombia today are the commercial work of Hollywood. In comparison to these Hollywood movies, all Colombian productions are low-budget films of low technical quality. Consequently, the success of Colombian film directors is generally limited and fleeting.

THEATER

Theatrical activity has been quite vibrant in Colombia in recent years. Avant-garde and experimental theater groups have placed Colombian theater within the league of contemporary drama in Latin America, Europe, and the United States since the late 1970s. Historically, Colombian theater has roots in indigenous performance arts, with a tradition from the colonial period to the present, including the work of one of Latin America's most prominent playwrights, Enrique Buenaventura.

Accounts from Spanish chroniclers point to the existence of a vibrant oral tradition among the Muiscas and other indigenous groups upon the arrival of the Spaniards in the sixteenth century. This oral tradition included ritualistic activities similar to Western theatrical performance, with choral music and dance. These rituals were frequently related to death, and women were involved far more than in premodern rituals in the West. There were also reports of the Muiscas doing theater-like performances of their religious-mythical stories when the Spaniards arrived in the sixteenth century. The Guajira Indians also had a strong performance tradition intact that included a significant dancing component.

During the colonial period, Spain brought the same Medieval and Renaissance theatrical traditions to be found in much of Latin America: religious works that often related the life of saints. The first Spanish play to be presented in Colombia was *Los Alarcos* (author unknown) in 1580. There is a written record of other plays, such as Hernando de Ospina's *La comedia de la guerra de los pijaos*, which dates back to the seventeenth century.

The first play to be presented in Colombia that has survived as a text is *Laura crítica* (1629), a satirical work with caricatures of social types by Fernando Fernández de Valenzuela. Fernández de Valenzuela wrote two other works in the seventeenth century, *Vida de hidalgos* and *En Dios está la vida*, both of unknown dates. These and other works of the colonial period were generally imitative of Spanish theater and had little to do with the local reality of New Granada.

In the late eighteenth and early nineteenth centuries, a national theater began to take form. Tomás Ramírez built and operated the Coliseo Ramírez, where thirty-nine plays were presented from 1792 to 1795. Later becoming the Teatro Colón, it has been Colombia's center for theater and the performing arts in the twentieth century.

The two major playwrights of the nineteenth century were José Fernández Madrid and Luis Vargas Tejada. Both were interested in attempting to do justice to the indigenous groups that had been displaced and massacred during the colonial period. Fernández Madrid produced at least two known works of this type: *Atalá* (1820) and *Tuatimocín* (date unknown). Vargas Tejada wrote many more plays dealing with a variety of topics, including indigenous themes and the satire of local customs.

During the second half of the nineteenth century, Colombian theater fell into a period of decadence. Most of the theater consisted of frivolous spectacles from Spain, usually *zarzuelas* and other forms of light humor. What appeared on the stages of Bogotá were often little more than circus spectacles with trapeze artists and the like.

Some Colombian playwrights did attempt to produce theater in the late nineteenth century, and the most noteworthy among these were José María Vergara y Vergara and Candelario Obeso. Vergara y Vergara was active in a variety of literary endeavors in the nineteenth century, and produced the play *El espíritu del siglo* (1896). Candelario Obeso was Colombia's first Afro-Colombian playwright, producing a work titled *Secudino el personero* (date unknown).

In the first half of the twentieth century, theater was a relatively weak genre with uneven production. However, during the early part of the century, the two most active playwrights, Lorenzo Marroquín and José Manuel Rivas Groot, were making strides in a modernist direction. Marroquin's *Lo irremediable* (1905) was representative of a new theater, with well-rounded characters of some psychological complexity. The theater of Marroquín and Rivas Groot had a new upper middle-class public that attended theater as an important social custom.

Early twentieth-century Colombian theater was also the scenario for describing social customs in a realist-naturalist mode. The two most prominent playwrights working along these lines were Max Grillo and Jacinto Albarracín. Grillo's *Vida nueva* (date unknown) describes the plight of rural *campesinos* and their difficulties in surviving as agricultural workers. An urban variant in this realist-naturalist mode was *Sol de diciembre* (1925) by Víctor Martínez Rivas, which was set in Bogotá with characters representing its customs.

Colombian theater entered a period of decadence from the 1930s to the 1950s, with relatively little theatrical activity—and of generally low quality. The exceptions to this generalization were the playwrights Antonio Alvarez Lleras and Luis Enrique Osorio. They were the first playwrights in Colombia to attempt to write and produce theater as a full-time profession. Alvarez Lleras wrote many plays from the 1920s to the 1950s, most of which were critical of middle-class social mores.

In the 1950s, Colombian theater became an increasingly vital cultural force and increasingly professionalized. A new theater of innovation and experimentation was evident by the 1960s, but the roots of this new attitude toward theater and experimental desire can be found in a few specific efforts dating back to the 1940s and 1950s. In Bogotá, these efforts were spearheaded by Marino Lemus López and Alvaro Zea Hernández. Similar initiatives were taken in Barranquilla by Amira de la Rosa (later by Alfredo de la Espriella) and in Tolima by Salvador Mesa Nicholls. Consequently, Colombians were able to see presentations of contemporary theater from Europe and the United States in Bogotá, Barranquilla, and Tolima, as well as avant-garde Colombian works.

The experimental movement took hold most visibly, however, in Cali in the 1950s. In 1953, Octavio Marulanda founded a group called Artistas del Pueblo; it later changed its name to Teatro Escuela de Cali (TEC) and has survived under the same initials, but is now called Teatro Experimental de Cali, headed by Enrique Buenaventura. In addition to the TEC, the Teatro Estudio de la Universidad del Valle also questioned the old guard of theater in Colombia.

In the mid–1950s, the group El Buho performed avant-garde theater in Colombia and abroad; they specialized in foreign theatrical production. Santiago García, who became prominent in the 1970s, began his work with El Buho. They also produced a play by Gonzalo Arango—better known in Colombia for his iconoclastic poetry. Arango and his generation of writers and artists, in fact, spearheaded a movement of *nadaísmo* in the 1960s that attempted to ridicule and undermine many Colombian cultural values that they considered too conventional and, in some cases, too provincial. They were interested in foreign theater, not because it was foreign, but because it was unconventional and, viewed in Colombia, quite iconoclastic (see chapter 6). These rebellious writers and artists shared some of the attitudes of the "Beat" generation in the United States.

After continued experimentation in the 1960s, Colombian theater assumed a mature role in Colombia in the 1970s, at the same time that it was reorganized internationally for the first time. In the early 1970s, Enrique Buenaventura found international recognition with *A la diestra de Dios Padre*, based on a story by Tomás Carrasquilla. This work has become a modern classic in Colombia and Latin America, having undergone several versions. Buenaventura has become the dean of Colombian playwrights, as well as one of Latin America's most recognized directors. He found the historical roots for his "new theater" in the Spanish playwright Lope de Vega's *El arte nuevo de hacer comedias*. Buenaventura cites parallels in matters such as theatrical movement, a new relationship with the audience, and a foundation of new poetics. Strongly affected by the theories of Brecht, Buenaventura strives for a politically active and intellectually engaged spectator; he has also used theater to heighten social and political awareness.

Buenaventura's TEC has also worked toward a theater free of European ("colonial") masters. Consequently, they have taken Latin American stories, poems, myths, and the like to create their own "Latin American" dramaturgy. In the TEC, the actors frequently offer their improvised response to these Latin American texts. In this new theater, the actor is freed from the "tyranny" of the playwright.

Besides Buenaventura's Teatro Experimental de Cali, the other major theater groups in Colombia in the 1970s were: the Teatro La Candelaria, the Teatro Popular de Bogotá (TPB), and the Teatro la Mama (extension of the group with the same name in New York). Santiago García provided the leadership for the Teatro La Candelaria, which produced both modern European theater and Colombian works. One of the most successful works was *I Took Panama*, a satirical look at Colombia's loss of Panama early in the twentieth century. Hugely successful in Colombia, *I Took Panama* is a humorous review of the historical record relating to Panama. The TPB and Teatro la Mama tended to follow the same pattern. The Casa de la Cultura was the sponsor of Carlos José Reyes's *Soldados*, a work based on Alvaro Cepeda Samudio's novel *La casa grande*, dealing with the government massacre of banana workers in 1928.

Contemporary Colombian theater has benefitted enormously from a theater festival held annually in Manizales. The most avant-garde and politically committed theater groups throughout Latin America have come to Colombia to perform in this festival, and it always attracts numerous Colombian theater groups to Manizales, from beginning amateur collections to the most sophisticated professionals.

In the 1990s, there have been more than two hundred amateur, semiprofessional and professional theater companies active in Colombia. Enrique Buenaventura and Santiago García remain the leading playwrights and directors in Colombia. More recently, Miguel Torres has had success in presenting work dealing with the takeover of the Palace of Justice, although Torres makes the historical event a part of the background to his play.

MUSIC

Colombia is a major player in the Latin American music world; the Colombian music industry is competitive in the international marketplace. The most popular and widespread Colombian music has African and Caribbean origins, and is associated primarily with the Costa region of Colombia. Afro-Caribbean rhythms also predominate in the western Pacific region; the Colombian center for Caribbean *salsa*, in fact, is the western city of Cali. In greater Antioquia and the interior highland regions, music has more Spanish origins and indigenous influence.

Traditional Colombian music has roots that correspond to the same regional divisions of numerous other facets of Colombian society and culture. In the interior highland, traditional music includes the *bambuco*, the *pasillo*, and the *guabina*. On the western coast, the *currulao*, the *contradanza*, and the *bamboleo* are the traditional music forms. The *joropo* and the *galerón* have the same role in the *llanos* (plains). In the Costa, the *vallenato, cumbia, porro, bullerengue, mapalé, garabato, puya*, and *fondongo* are the most representative musical forms.

In the 1980s, Nobel Laureate Gabriel García Márquez contributed to the national and international popularity of the *vallenato* music of the Caribbean coast. This Afro-Colombian music was named after Valledupar, the capital of the northern Caribbean department of El César. An upbeat and quick-rhythmed accordion music with direct connections to the oral tradition of the Caribbean coast, the *vallenato* has roots that have been traced back to the *merengue* of the Dominican Republic in the mid–nineteenth century. By the late nineteenth and early twentieth centuries, *vallenato* music as it is known today had taken form, being played by traveling troubadours who moved from one small town to another on the Caribbean coast, providing one of the few sources of news in a region where national newspapers did not circulate until the 1930s. The topics of *vallenatos*, however, vary considerably, covering themes related to work, the natural setting, local and national politicians, local flora and fauna, and the like. With the advent of modern musical technology, the *vallenato* has evolved considerably from its origins in traditional oral cultures of the Caribbean coast. In the 1940s, *vallenato* songs of the most famous singers, such as Rafael Escalona, were first recorded as records available for commercial sale. By the 1960s and 1970s, *vallenatos* were readily available on both disks and cassettes. In the 1990s, Carlos Vives has been an international celebrity throughout the Hispanic world, singing *vallenatos* that draw upon the tradition of this song form, but also using the latest musical technology, adding a slight rock rhythm and electronic musical instruments to produce *vallenatos* widely heard and appreciated in all of Latin America, as well as Spain and in the Hispanic sectors of the United States. With the addition of the electric and acoustic guitar, drums, and flutes, Vives has made the *vallenato* a music beat for dancing throughout the Hispanic world.

In the 1980s and 1990s, *vallenatos* surpassed the *cumbia* in popularity. *Vallenatos* are representative of the triethnic and oral culture of the Caribbean coastal region. Given his own interests in oral and multiethnic cultures, García Márquez's lifetime fascination with the *vallenato* is understandable. In fact, he once claimed that his novel, *One Hundred Years of Solitude*, is nothing more than a 350-page *vallenato*.

Before the *vallenato*, the most widely known music of the Caribbean coast was the *cumbia*, another quick-rhythmed Afro-Colombian music generally more frivolous in content than the *vallenato*. *Cumbias* are usually love songs about relationships, or songs about festivities, parties, or dancing itself. In fact, the Colombian *cumbia* has been a classic standby for dancing at Latin American festivities for the past several decades. Over the years, there has been much speculation by both amateurs and experts about the origin of the word *cumbia*, which has been attributed to both indigenous and African sources. Some of the most informed linguists have suggested that the *cumbia* could have origins in both of these potential sources, and with most direct connections to an African dialect brought to Colombia. In any case, many of Colombia's best-known popular artists have been composers or singers of *cumbias*. When Gabriel García Márquez received the Nobel Prize for Literature in 1982, he and his wife danced to the *cumbia* "La cumbia cieneguera" at the ceremony, with music composed by Andrés Paz Barros and words by Humberto Daza Granados.

The *bolero* transcends regional boundaries in Colombia, and has provided the standard (highly romanticized) love songs for Colombians since the 1940s. Histories of the *bolero* generally attribute its birth in Cuba during the nineteenth century, with early precedents in Puerto Rico and Mexico, as well. In Colombia, the *bolero* dates back to 1919.

The pioneer of the *bolero* in Colombia was Daniel Lemaitre, a successful businessman in Cartagena early in the twentieth century who turned to music as a second career with enormous success. He was interested in various types of popular music, but was actually the creator of the first *bolero* in Colombia, "Niña de ojos azules," in 1919. Since there was no technology in Colombia to record it, this *bolero* remained a memory among friends and musicians in the region. Some of his other *boleros* were: "Con el amor no se juega," "Como las olas," "Amor callado," "Tú vives en mí," and "La ventanita."

The "golden age" of *bolero* in Colombia was from the 1940s to the 1960s (roughly the same period that the *bolero* was equally popular throughout Latin America). Most Colombians associate the *bolero* with Cuban music of the 1940s and 1950s. Nevertheless, Colombia produced some 1,250 *boleros* in the twentieth century, most of which have been composed by musicians from the Costa. Colombians have created their own variant of the *bolero*, the romantic *bolero vallenato*. Alfredo Gutiérrez and Calixto Ochoa have composed now classic *boleros vallenatos*. Diomedes Díaz and his group, the Binomio de Oro, have sung *boleros vallenatos* with great popular and commercial success in Colombia. During the 1940s, Rafael Escalona cut a series of records that circulated nationally, as did Alejo Durán.

Among the numerous cultivators of the *bolero* in Colombia, the most renowned are: Jorge Añez Avendaño, Efraín Orozco Morales, Francisco Galán Blanco (known as "Pacho Galán"), Bonifacio Bautista Gálvez, Rafael Roncallo Vilar, Luis Eduardo Bermúdez Acosta (known as "Lucho Bermúdez"), Esthercita Forero, José A. Morales, Leonor Buenaventura de Valencia, José Barros, Luis Uribe Bueno, Lino Ibáñez, Ignacio Dugando Roncalles (known as "Nacho Dugand"), Jaime R. Echavarría, Jorge Villamil Cordóvez, Graciela Arango de Tabón, Mario Gareña, Héctor Ulloa (known as "El Chinche Ulloa"), Víctor Manuel García Cuadros (known as "Manoello"), Flavio Santador Lora (known as "Kike Santander"), and Fabio Salgado Mejía (known as "Estéfano").

Among these modern composers of the *bolero*, Lucho Bermúdez (1912–1994) was one of the most productive in a variety of musical forms, writing *porros*, *cumbias*, *gaitas*, and *pasillos*. He had numerous hit records in several genres. His *boleros*, such as "La vida es así," "Llorando una pena," and "Embeleso," are not that well known by the general public in Colombia.

José Barros (born in 1915) came from a markedly impoverished background and has spent much of his life in a variety of subsistence-level jobs while attempting to make a living composing popular songs. In the process, he has experimented with everything from *boleros* to *tangos*. In the mid–1950s, he created one of the most popular songs in Colombia for many years, "La Piragua."

Nacho Dugand (born in 1922 in Barranquilla) has been one of Colombia's most prolific *bolero* composers, creating more than 150 from the 1940s to the 1990s. In the 1940s, he composed romantic *boleros*, such as "Pensando en ti," "Pechiche," and "Añorada." One of his classic tunes from the 1950s was "Pincelada" (1955). Dugand's *boleros* from the 1960s included "A unos ojos" (1960), "Te acordarás de mí" (1962), "Antioquia" (1965), and "A lo mejor" (1968). His more recent works include "Soy colombiano" (1987) and "Recuerdos" (1992).

Graciela Arango de Tobón (born in Oveja in 1932) has composed *boleros*, *bambucos*, *cumbias*, *merengues*, *porros*, *paseos*, *pasillos*, and *baladas*. Her biggest hit was "Qué es amor?" (1975), which was sung by several singers, and in the 1990s by María Cristina in her album *20 boleros colombianos*.

"El Chinche Ulloa" (born in La Vega in 1938) has composed several superb *boleros*, the most popular of them being "Cinco centavitos," which was a hit in both Colombia and other Latin American countries. He also composed the *boleros* "Aunque me duela," "El traje blanco," and "Balance."

"Manoello" (born in Cali, 1948) has composed more than two-hundred songs, including *boleros*, *cumbias*, country tunes, rock `n' roll songs, and *vallenatos*. His most popular *bolero*, which he both composed and sang himself, was "Hablemos." His other best-known *boleros* are "Cuando pienso que no estás,"

"Este amor," (both sung by Claudia de Colombia), "Cuando te hablen de mí" (sung by Diana María), and "Te llevo dentro de mí" (sung by Gustavo Gil).

"Kike Santander" (born in Cali in 1960) has become one of Colombia's most prominent musical figures in the 1990s. As a youth, he was interested in *salsa* and jazz. On the basis of his success in composing songs in Colombia, he was invited to Miami, where he began work for Sony. Eventually, he began composing music for Gloria Estefan. In addition, he has composed *boleros* and *cumbias* that have won awards in competitions in Mexico and the United States.

"Estéfano" (born in Manizales in 1967) has also been quite successful in the United States. His *bolero* "Mi tierra" was awarded a Grammy in 1996, and his song "Mi buen amor" was enormously successful in the United States. His *bolero* "Te juro que me haces falta" was also recorded by Sony.

In the 1990s, the *bolero* experienced a comeback in Colombia, with some radio stations dedicated exclusively to the playing of *boleros*. The international resurgence of this music is signaled by the fact that celebrity figures of other genres, such as the opera singer Plácido Domingo, have sung *boleros*.

Finally, Colombia has been developing a nascent rock music scene in recent decades. Generally speaking, the venues for rock music are quite limited in Colombia, for there is relatively little public space open for young rock groups to become established. In addition, the situation in Colombian rock is somewhat comparable to that of Colombian film: both are so overshadowed by their counterparts in the United States that even survival is difficult. Despite these difficulties, rock music with strong American and Colombian elements, sung in Spanish, can be heard in Colombia. In the 1970s, the group "Génesis" recorded hit songs in Colombia by combining traditional Colombian music with rock music. The group, which consisted of musicians Edgar Restrepo, Juan Fernando Echavarría, Beatriz Vargas, Mario García, and Humberto Monroy, was at its apogee from 1972 to 1976, and in the 1990s recorded some of its old hits on CD with most of the original group and one new member.

In the 1990s, rock music made a comeback in Colombia, with increased support on commercial radio and more opportunities to play in public. This is particularly the case of Medellín, which has become something of a center for rock music in Colombia. One of the most successful rock groups in Colombia in the 1990s was "Aterciopelados," with lead singer Andrea Echeverri. Other professional rock groups are "Bailo y Conspiro," "Estados Alterados," "La Derecha," "1.280 Almas," "Neurosis," and "La Pestilencia."

Music is important in the daily life of Colombians in all regions. Nevertheless, the city of Cali is particularly well known for its lively nightlife, dancing, and music. More specifically, Cali has become a center for Caribbean *salsa* in

Colombia. Originally from Cuba and Puerto Rico, *salsa* dates back to the 1920s and 1930s. Today, music historians of the Caribbean speak of the "old guard" of *salsa* from the 1940s to the 1960s, and the new, urban *salsa* dating from the 1960s, with its centers in New York and Puerto Rico. This new, urban *salsa* was being produced throughout Colombia in the 1970s by groups such as "Fruko y sus tesoros" in Medellín, "Piper Pimienta" in Cali, "Los Latin Brothers" in Barranquilla, and "Willi Salcedo" in Bogotá. In recent decades, however, the *salsa* movement has been growing in Cali, fomented by regular tours of the top *salsa* bands from New York and Puerto Rico. In 1986, the Puerto Rican Raphy Leavitt, director of the group "La Selecta," claimed that the strongest *salsa* market in the world, even stronger than in New York or Puerto Rico, was in Cali.

In the 1980s, Cali surfaced as a center for *salsa*, led by the musical productions of the "Grupo Niche," which has competed internationally with the best *salsa* groups from throughout the Caribbean. At first, many Colombians assumed that the "Grupo Niche" was a new musical group from Puerto Rico. In reality, the band was put together by friends from the Chocó region, just north of Cali. Their first record had limited commercial success, but since then they have developed a large following in Cali and beyond, including the production of hit records. Their music uses a *salsa* beat, but the lyrics come from their roots on the Pacific coast of Colombia. In general, musicians from Cali have not gained international reputations, but professional *salsa* dancers from Cali have fared well in international competition. Locally, modern dance groups perform *salsa* as part of their repertoire.

Besides the "Grupo Niche," some thirty-five *salsa* groups have arisen in Cali since the 1980s. Most of the musicians in these groups are from the area, with a few foreigners from the Caribbean region. The contact between these Colombian musicians and the foreigners has contributed even more to the development of *salsa* in Cali. In the 1970s, some Colombian bands played a variety of Caribbean tunes that included *salsa*. Groups such as "La Gran Banda Caleña" and "Los Bunkers" operated in this fashion. Groups that have arisen since the 1980s playing exclusively *salsa* include "La Cali Charanga," "El Grupo Bembé," and "Eco Antillano." More recently, there has been an experimental movement of groups working on the margins of mainline *salsa*. These counterculture musicians, who have added new energy to the *salsa* scene in Cali, are "Latin Jazz," "Areíto," and "La Charanga Latina."

The cultural phenomenon of *salsa* has had such an impact in Cali and on Colombian culture in general that there have already been scholarly studies dedicated to this matter. For example, it has been noted that more international *salsa* groups (such as Puerto Rican Bobby Valentín, Melcochita from

New York, and a group from Caracas) have dedicated songs to the city of Cali than any other city, including New York or San Juan, Puerto Rico. Social scientists have speculated exactly why the phenomenon of *salsa* has taken place in Cali. On one hand, they point to the strong African cultural heritage in Cali, and the obvious cultural links to the Caribbean, which was the original center of African slave trade. On the other hand, they have suggested that the urban development of Cali since the 1920s has made it propitious for musical activity. At the same time, the role of the media has been significant, particularly in the ability of radio and television to connect Cali culturally with the Caribbean.

In summary, Colombian music is rich and varied in accordance with the regional traditions from which it has arisen. The music from the Caribbean coast with strong influences from Caribbean music in general, such as the *vallenato* and the *cumbia* have had the most impact beyond the borders of Colombia. In addition two music forms basically imported from Caribbean neighbors—the *bolero* and *salsa*—have been appropriated in Colombia and are flourishing. These song forms, in fact, have been most important in providing Colombia with a significant role on the international music map.

6

Literature

Colombia has enjoyed a venerable tradition in belles lettres, and most Colombians take great pride in this tradition. Educated Colombians consider their nation a stronghold of literature and the arts, and are especially proud of their country's poetic tradition. Since the turn of the twentieth century, in fact, Colombians have referred to Bogotá as the "Athens of South America." Numerous Colombian presidents and many of its statesmen were men of letters—a tradition that extends back to Miguel Antonio Caro and Marco Fidel Suárez, distinguished scholars who also served as presidents. Among the recent presidents, liberal Alfonso López Michelsen published a novel and several books of essays before becoming president, and Conservative Belisario Betancur was a published poet who also had written numerous books of essays before becoming his party's candidate for the presidency. Since the colonial period, the cultivation of literature has been considered not only a sign of education, but also of refinement and even aristocracy. Consequently, literature has not only been the arena of professional writers, but also of amateur authors who view writing as a method of attaining or confirming class credentials—as well as a passport into politics, diplomacy, or the cultural bureaucracy.

Historically, Colombia has not had publishing houses as large and competitive as those found in nations such as Argentina and Mexico. Nevertheless, the nation has produced at least one major writer in each of the major periods of Latin American history: the chronicler Juan Rodríguez Freyle in the colonial period, romantic poet and novelist Jorge Isaacs in the nineteenth century, and Nobel Laureate Gabriel García Márquez in the twentieth century. Several other Colombian writers, such as José Eustacio Rivera and Alvaro Mutis, are widely recognized in the Hispanic world.

In the 1970s and 1980s, the boom of the Latin American novel, as well as the international celebrity of García Márquez and his receiving the Nobel Prize led to a renewed vitality of the Colombian novel. Many young writers dedicated themselves to work on novels, and the concurrent rise of the publishing industry created a Colombian "mini-boom," in which several younger writers, such as Gustavo Alvarez Gardeazábal and R. H. Moreno-Durán, were widely read and recognized in Colombia. At the same time, these writers and many of their cohorts had to deal with writing under the "shadow" of García Márquez.

In any society, the idea of surviving as a professional writer is always problematic at best, and throughout most of Colombia's history it has generally been impossible. In the nineteenth century, literature was basically the weekend hobby of men of letters, whose primary occupation was typically politics, business, or overseeing their plantations. Women married to men in these social positions also had the luxury of writing; indeed, one of the most prolific novelists of the nineteenth century was Soledad Acosta de Samper, an accomplished writer married to one of Colombia's major political and intellectual figures, José María Samper. There were no publishing houses in the modern sense in Colombia until the mid–twentieth century. Rather, there were printers who printed books commissioned (and paid) by the writers themselves. Consequently, much of the "literature" that appears in the histories of Colombian literature was originally published in printings of only three hundred to five hundred copies.

Most of the publishers in Colombia today would be classified as "small presses" in the United States; a typical printing of a novel from the 1960s to the 1990s (other than García Márquez) has been a run of only two to three thousand copies. For this and other reasons, aspiring writers in Colombia have always had to find another means of economic subsistence while they write. Most novelists and poets in Colombia today work on their books part-time, making their livelihood as journalists or part-time professors, and most of them combine two or three sources of income as a method of continuing their creative efforts. Occasionally, writers other than García Márquez have found enough economic security in writing to dedicate themselves full-time for a year or two exclusively to their chosen profession. Novelists Manuel Mejía Vallejo, Gustavo Alvarez Gardeazábal, and David Sánchez Juliao, for example, have had periods of full-time writing because of their novel sales. In the mid–1990s, however, Alvarez Gardeazábal became a full-time politician and Sánchez Juliao a diplomat.

Writers Manuel Mejía Vallejo, Alonso Aristizábal, and Fanny Buitrago

HISTORICAL BACKGROUND

Spanish control of intellectual activity and the writer's isolation were predominant factors during the colonial period. The publication of literature and distribution of novels printed in Spain was prohibited. The writer's isolation can be attributed to several factors. The governmental and intellectual centers, such as Bogotá and Tunja, were geographically set apart. Men and women of letters were generally priests or officials of the Catholic Church's hierarchy who lived in the isolation of monasteries. Literary production of any sort, rigidly controlled by a political and ecclesiastic elite, was a privilege of a small minority.

The major work of narrative prose written during the colonial period was *El carnero* (*The Ram*, completed in 1638). One of the few colonial works still read in Colombia, *El carnero* is a historical chronicle of life in Santa Fe de Bogotá during a one hundred-year period, 1539–1636. A picaresque work, *El carnero* is a synthesis of war news, changes in government, customs, psychological portraits, adventure, scandal, crime, historical fact, and legends.

Nineteenth-century literature in Colombia followed a pattern similar to much of Latin America: During the independence movement and the early years of the republic, political essays and creative literature with neoclassical models dominated. Two generations of romantics, realists, and the first *modernistas* followed. By the second half of the nineteenth century, when literary culture was a more institutionalized activity than ever before, its center was Bogotá. José María Vergara y Vergara established in Bogotá a literary group identified as "El Mosaico," which published a magazine of the same name. Despite the predominance of the capital, the first Colombian novel was written in the Caribbean coastal region, and the major realist and *costumbrista* writers came from greater Antioquia. At the end of the nineteenth century, in fact, the national polemic was between the traditional *antioqueños* and the new modernists.

LITERATURE FROM THE CARIBBEAN COAST

The coastal region of Colombia has been geographically and culturally isolated from the interior throughout the nation's history. The region's key role in African slave trade resulted in a cultural and racial makeup notably different from the remainder of Colombia. The predominantly Hispanic Bogotá has stood in contrast with the culturally heterogeneous and markedly African coastal region. These cultural differences, in addition to other geographical, political, and economic factors have resulted in vital artistic and literary traditions that have generally been at a considerable aesthetic distance from the inland traditions.

Unlike the comparatively isolated and conservative cultural traditions of Bogotá and Medellín, the Barranquilla of the twentieth century was progressive, less traditional, and affected by foreign influences. Two renowned coastal poets, Candelario Obeso (1849–1884) and Luis Carlos López (1883–1950) brought to Colombian verse colloquial language and popular themes. Ramón Vinyes, a Spaniard from Catalonia, in effect brought modern European literature and the latest avant-garde trends to Colombia by publishing the cultural magazine *Voces* from 1917 to 1920. During the 1940s and 1950s, the writer José Félix Fuenmayor (1885–1966) functioned as a literary father figure for the group of young artists and intellectuals later to be designated as the "Group of Barranquilla." This group included: the painter Alejandro Obregón (see chapter 8), writers Gabriel García Márquez (see chapter 7) and Alvaro Cepeda Samudio (1926–1972), journalist Alfonso Fuenmayor (1927–1992), and journalist/critic Germán Vargas. The Barranquilla newspaper *El Heraldo* has played a vital role in coastal culture since the 1940s, regularly publishing the writing of García Márquez and other members of the group.

Colombia's first novelist, Juan José Nieto (1804–1866), from Cartagena, was also one of Colombia's major political and military leaders of the nineteenth century. His novel *Ingermina* (1844) is generally considered the first novel to be published in Colombia. (Nevertheless, it has not been republished in the twentieth century and is only available in special collections of libraries; the "classic" nineteenth-century novel that most Colombians read is *María* by Jorge Isaacs.) *Ingermina* is a historical novel set in the sixteenth century and deals with the conquest of the Calamar Indians. Nieto also developed a love story, and intercalated descriptions and local customs. *Los moriscos* (1845), Nieto's second novel, deals with the expulsion of the Moors from Spain. Both novels offer clichéd character potrayals, weakly developed plots, and simplistic narrative techniques.

The tradition of Afro-American poetry initiated by Candelario Obeso is continued in the twentieth century by Jorge Artel (1905). His most important work, *Tambores en la noche* (*Drums in the Night*, 1940), integrates folklore of the African-Caribbean culture, particularly the tone and rhythms of this culture's music. Artel's poetry contains less linguistic imitation than Obeso's, and the sea is a constant presence, both as theme and generator of rhythm.

Two other twentieth-century poets from this region are Gregorio Castañeda Aragón (born 1886) and Meira Delmar (pseudonym of Olga Champs, born 1921). Castañeda Aragón, from Santa Marta, wrote extensively from 1916 to 1959, publishing nine books of poetry, mostly dealing with popular themes in a nostalgic tone. Meira Delmar of Barranquilla has written poetry closely tied to the sea and her Middle Eastern cultural heritage. She has published more than six books of poetry from the 1940s to the 1990s.

During the 1920s, Barranquilla's new middle class was beginning to thrive and the appearance of the modern novel accompanied this change. The initiators were José Félix Fuenmayor and Manuel García Herreros (1894–1950). Both were of the generation of writers in Barranquilla who had witnessed the publication of the magazine *Voces*. Fuenmayor's novel, *Cosme* (1927), is one of the most important novels of the twentieth century. It played a key role in the development of modern fiction in Colombia as a direct predecessor to the new novel that would appear in the 1950s. *Cosme* is the story of a protagonist by this name and his life in Barranquilla. The irreverent attitude toward traditional institutions (including literary institutions), ironic tone, and humor make *Cosme* an exception in comparison to the main trends of Colombian and Latin American fiction of the time. The urban environment and alienated protagonist also make it quite distinctive. Fuenmayor's second novel, *Una triste aventura de 14 sabios* (*A Sad Adventure of 14 Wise Men*, 1928), is science fiction dealing with a group of fourteen scholars and scientists who depart in a flying machine for an uninhabited island to carry out secret experiments. The earth expands enormously in size, but the travelers remain the same. Consequently, they return to find that what seems to them an enormous stone is actually a grain of sand. There is also a character who comments on this novel during the process of its development. The imaginative quality of *Una triste aventura de 14 sabios* is its outstanding feature and an important contribution to the coastal tradition.

García Herrero's relatively unknown novels, *Lejos del mar* (*Far from the Sea*, 1921) and *Asaltos* (*Assaults*, 1929), were more traditional than Fuenmayor's inventions. *Lejos del mar* is a short novel, narrated in first person, in which the protagonist nostalgically relates the story of a youth's maturation process in a small rural town.

The modern fiction initiated on the coast by José Félix Fuenmayor is continued on the coast by Alvaro Cepeda Samudio, Héctor Rojas Herazo (1921), and Gabriel García Márquez (see chapter 7).

LITERATURE OF GREATER ANTIOQUIA

Greater Antioquia has not been as geographically isolated from the remainder of the nation as the Caribbean coast. Nevertheless, this region (including the present-day states of Caldas and Quindío) has been willfully independent of the rest of the nation and quite often in direct opposition to it.

Upon gaining independence, Antioquia already had a well-established intellectual elite like that of Bogotá, Popayán, and Cartagena. Its literary production in the nineteenth century consisted of an unimpressive set of political speeches, patriotic poetry, and parochial essays. Antioquia's most renowned poet, Gregorio Gutiérrez González (1826–1872), led the typical life of the landowner of this region: he grew up in the country (in a small town, La Ceja), studied law in Bogotá, and later returned to his native province. While in Bogotá, he wrote romantic poetry and in 1866 published the lengthy and at times prosaic poem *Memorial científica sobre el cultivo del maíz en los climas cálidos del Estado de Antioquia por uno de los miembros de la Escuela de Ciencias; Artes; dedicado a la misma Escuela* (*Scientific Memoir on the Cultivation of Corn in the Warm Climate of the State of Antioquia by One of the Members of the School of Sciences; Arts; Dedicated to the Same School*). Written in the popular language of the region, this poem is a detailed and realistic description of the agriculture and land of Antioquia, as well as a celebration of working the land.

Economic growth in greater Antioquia in the late nineteenth century was accompanied by an outburst of literary production that continued through the twentieth century. The first major novelist of the region, Tomás Carrasquilla (1858–1940), typifies the middle-class Antioquian writer who did not belong to the elite that had dominated Colombian literature up to the twentieth century. Of modest social background, Carrasquilla produced realist and costumbrista fiction in considerable volume between 1896 and 1935. Most of it was nostalgic in tone, evoking an idyllic, rural past that was vanishing in the twentieth century. His three major novels were *Frutos de mi tierra* (*Fruits of My Land*, 1896), *Grandeza* (*Greatness*, 1910), and *La marquesa de Yolombó* (*The Marquise of Yolombó*, 1926). In contrast with the cosmopolitan tastes of the turn-of-the-century *modernistas*—mostly elitist writers from Bogotá—Carrasquilla defended a realist-naturalist approach to the description of human beings in their environment.

In the nineteenth century, literary language in Antioquia was dominated by popular speech. Poet Porfirio Barba Jacob (pseudonym of Miguel Angel Osorio, 1883–1942) modified this practice at the beginning of the twentieth century. Traces of the language of modernism in Barba Jacob's early poetry represented a break from the Antioquian tradition of popular literary language. A more radical innovation of Colombian verse arrived with the poetry of León de Greiff (1895–1976), a key figure of the Los Nuevos group of writers based primarily in Bogotá.

Antioquia also participated in the next generation's movement for a modern literature, that associated with the magazine *Mito* (*Myth*, 1955–1962). Rogelio Echavarría was Antioquia's representative with *Mito*, virtually the only outlet for free creative expression published during the dictatorship of Rojas Pinilla during the 1950s. Rogelio Echavarría's direction as a poet was present in his first book *Edad sin tiempo* (*Age without Time*, 1948): use of modern imagery, precise language, sobriety, and moderation.

The novel in twentieth-century Antioquia has generally been more traditional than the poetry of the likes of León de Greiff. During the 1920s and 1930s, fiction of the regionalist and social vein was predominant. The first truly modern novel to be published in Antioquia was Manuel Mejía Vallejo's *El día señalado* (*The Appointed Day*, 1964). Fiction in the Antioquian tradition culminates with the modern novels of Mejía Vallejo.

LITERATURE OF THE INTERIOR HIGHLAND

Bogotá and the interior highland region surrounding it have been privileged cultural centers since the colonial period and dominant in all aspects of literary production since Colombia's independence. "Culture" in this region's context refers to the literary culture produced by the elite since the colonial period: The region's indigenous population was decimated and highland culture has been predominantly Hispanic. Bogotá and Tunja were centers of literary activity during the colonial period.

In the nineteenth century, the "novel of customs" was quite popular, and its primary exponents in the interior highland region were Eugenio Díaz (1804–1865), Luis Segundo Silvestre (1838–1887), Soledad Acosta de Samper (1833–1913), José Manuel Groot (1800–1878), and José Manuel Marroquín (1827–1908). Eugenio Díaz's *Manuela* (1858) first appeared in Vergara y Vergara's *El mosaico* and contained numerous descriptions of the local setting and customs of the town and region. Nevertheless, it was an early example of the rural social protest novel and, unlike the provincial novels of customs, was national in vision.

Nineteenth-century poetic language in the highlands was dominated by the romantic verse of Rafael Pombo (1833–1912). Pombo was a prolific poet whose language developed and changed over the second half of the nineteenth century. His acquaintance with English poets and study of the classics late in his career resulted in a more heterogeneous poetry than his sometimes simplistic early romanticism. Joaquín González Camargo (1865–1886) also wrote romantic poetry, published posthumously as *Poesías* (*Poetry*; 1889).

Miguel Antonio Caro and José Asunción Silva were representatives of opposite tendencies of poetic language at the turn of the century in Bogotá. Caro was the central figure, with Rufino José Cuervo and Marco Fidel Suárez, in the humanist movement strongly rooted in Hispanic classic tradition. (At the same time, Caro was an early example of the man of letters in Colombia who also served as statesman and even president; as such, he was a direct predecessor of recent Presidents Alfonso López Michelsen and Belisario Betancur.) Caro's poetry is one of ideas rather than emotion; his odes and sonnets often have the academic tone to be expected of the translator of Virgil and the scholar that Caro was. Silva, in contrast, had as his sources Baudelaire, Verlaine, Rimbaud, Poe, and other nineteenth-century Europeans. Silva's poetic language is vague, musical, and suggestive.

In the twentieth century, several generations of poets have left their mark on Colombia's venerable poetic tradition. In the 1920s, the most important highland representative of the group Los Nuevos was Germán Pardo García (born 1902), author of some thirty books of poetry. During the mid–1930s, the Piedra y Cielo group of poets—Arturo Camacho Ramírez (born 1910), Eduardo Carranza (born 1913), Tomás Vargas Osorio (born 1908), Jorge Rojas (born 1911), and Darío Samper (born 1913)—began to establish a literary identity in Bogotá. They renovated Colombian poetry, using as their models the Spaniards Juan Ramón Jiménez and Federico García Lorca, as well as the Chilean Pablo Neruda. Much of their poetry was an avant-garde search for metaphor for the sake of metaphor. In the mid–1940s, a group consisting of Fernando Charry Lara (born 1920), Alvaro Mutis (born 1923), Eduardo Varela (born 1918), and others became identified with the name "Cántico," after the Spaniard Jorge Guillén's book of that title. The poets associated with the magazine *Mito* were the dominant force in the 1950s: Jorge Gaitán Durán (1924–1962), Eduardo Cote Lemus (1928–1964), Carlos Obregón (1929–1965), Carlos Castro Saavedra (born 1924), Julio José Fajardo (born 1919), Dora Castellanos (born 1925), Jorge Eliécer Ruiz (born 1931), and Octavio Gamboa (born 1923). Gaitán Durán and Hernando Valencia Goelkel founded *Mito* in 1955, with the following statement as a kind of doctrine for the generation: "Words are in their situation. It would be vain to demand for them univocal or ideal position . . . In order to accept them in their ambiguity, we need words *to be*." The generation of *Mito* was short-lived as a group because of the premature deaths of two of its most accomplished poets, Gaitán Durán and Cote Lemus.

The twentieth-century novel in the interior highland region was the fiction of official literary language, as opposed to the popular traditions of greater Antioquia and the oral tradition of the Caribbean coast. For example, the novels and political positions of José Manuel Marroquín and Angel Cuervo were conservative and traditional. Lorenzo Marroquín (1856–1918) and José María Rivas Groot (1863–1923) coauthored *Pax* (1907), a novel criticized by conservatives (because they were satirized in it), but which nevertheless fulfilled the same fundamentally patriotic function of much conservative turn-of-the-century fiction.

The irreverent iconoclast during these years of conservative domination was novelist José María Vargas Vila. Author of more than thirty novels and other writings, he was a vociferous opponent of the Catholic Church, and many of his novels were openly anti-clerical. Vargas Vila's often ungrammatical language placed him squarely in opposition to the conservative grammarians Caro and Cuervo. Indeed, the aesthetic quality of Vargas Vila's novels was uneven, but his most successful works, such as *Flor de fango* (*Flower of Mud*, 1895) and *La novena sinfonía* (*The Ninth Symphony*, 1928), have survived the test of time. Another fiction writer with extravagant aesthetic tastes, Clímaco Soto Borda, published *Polvo y ceniza* (*Dust and Ash*, 1906), a volume of stories printed with blue letters and type running the long dimension of the page. In addition, he wrote *Diana cazadora* (*Diana the Huntress*, 1915), a satire of the modernists.

In the 1930s, José A. Osorio Lizarazo became Colombia's writer of the proletariat, whose fiction arose out of this crisis of a changing society. In *La casa de vecindad* (*The Apartment House*, 1930), Osorio Lizarazo presents a narrator-protagonist's futile attempts to understand a technological society too complex for him. Each of Osorio Lizarazo's dozen novels communicates a proletariat impulse, even though the ideological implications of this fiction are not consistent.

Eduardo Zalamea Borda demonstrates interest in aesthetic concerns rather than ideological stances in *Cuatro años a bordo de mí mismo* (*Four Years with Myself*, 1934). It relates the journey of a youth from Bogotá to the coastal Guajira area. Modernity and technology function here not to demonstrate the circumstance of the proletariat, but to contrast the folkloric rural culture of the coast and the technological urban culture of Bogotá. The focus is on an individual's transition into manhood.

The novelistic production of the interior highland participates in a venerable tradition of literary culture which ranges in ideological content from the conservative writings of turn-of-the-century grammarians to the proletarian novels of Osorio Lizarazo. The culmination of this highland tradition of literature informed by writing culture (as opposed to popular culture or societal concerns) is to be found in the fiction of Eduardo Caballero Calderón. His major novel is *El buen salvaje* (1965), a self-conscious story of a young Colombian in Europe learning to be a writer.

LITERATURE OF GREATER TOLIMA

Greater Tolima, which includes the region of present-day Tolima and Huila, has been closely associated with Bogotá economically and the interior highland tradition culturally.[1] The reasons for this economic and cultural attachment have been numerous. The road between Bogotá and the town of Honda in Tolima has always served as the connecting land bridge for all river traffic from the Magdalena River destined for Bogotá. Railroad connection from Bogotá to Girardot and Puerto Salgar was also vitally important. During times of economic stagnation in the highlands, Bogotá's oligarchy has often taken land in the fertile *tierra caliente* (hot lowlands) of Tolima to undertake financial recovery. Tolima has been traditionally connected commerically with the highlands. Culturally, Tolima has looked to Bogotá as the "Athens of South America"—a model and center of intellectual activity.

Two major writers born in Tolima, José María Samper and José Eustacio Rivera (1889–1928), were associated with both this region and Bogotá. Samper was born in Honda, where he lived his youth. A consummate man of letters, Samper published voluminously. As a literary phenomenon himself and as part of the inner circle of Bogotá's *El mosaico*, Samper was the product and producer par excellence of the oligarchy's literary culture in nineteenth-century Tolima and the interior highland.

In the first quarter of the twentieth century, José Eustacio Rivera also moved from Tolima to Bogotá to assume a role comparable to Samper's: Samper's hyperproductivity was matched by Rivera's hyperaestheticism. Rivera's family did not belong to the wealthy elite; nevertheless, his parents were landowners who were active in the politics of the region now known as Huila. His early education and career were typical of the highland's future men of letters: He was educated in a private high school, began a career at the age of sixteen as an *escribiente* (scribe) in the government bureaucracy, studied later at the National University in Bogotá, and during his adulthood dedicated himself to intellectual pursuits after having taught in the Colegio de San Simón in Ibagué. Rivera is best known for his novel, *La vorágine* (*The Vortex*, 1924), a classic work of

Colombian and Latin American literature. It is the story of Arturo Cova, poet and decadent intellectual who travels into Colombia's jungle territory. Analysis of the function of the narrator in *La vorágine* demonstrates that Rivera was concerned with his role as intellectual in Colombian society when he wrote this classic novel in Colombian literature.[2]

The roles of authors, novels, and the reading public were still in many ways undefined and ambiguous in Colombia in 1924, when Rivera published *La vorágine*. It is appropriate to note, for example, that the first edition included a supposed photograph of the protagonist, Arturo Cova. *La vorágine* is not only a story of adventure and social injustice, but also about writing itself: Its ambiguities and contradictions are all part of a text striving to attain the status of a written text. Despite the often repeated assertion that all these early twentieth-century classic novels in Latin America—such as *La vorágine*—were simply variations on the same theme of "they were devoured by the jungle," *La vorágine* does not play out this pattern in a significant way. The most significant drama is not the death of protagonist Cova or anyone else, but rather the survival of the text. As such, *La vorágine* represents the expression of a now-mature literary culture in the Tolima and highlands region.

The civil war called La Violencia was particularly intense in the Tolima region, and it was the major sociopolitical event to affect writing in this region. La Violencia produced a vast literature, to a large extent very personal accounts of human suffering, often vivid in imagery but generally mediocre as an aesthetic experience. One outstanding exception to this generalization was *El jardín de las Hartmann* (*The Garden of the Hartmanns*, 1978) by Jorge Eliécer Pardo (1945), a well-wrought short novel dealing with the historical period of La Violencia in Tolima. The violent conflict appears in a relatively abstract fashion, without attaching political parties or names to the events, and avoiding gruesome accounts of bloody anecdotes. Pardo universalizes the conflict by creating a parallel between La Violencia and the anti-Nazi resistance in Germany.

The novels of Héctor Sánchez (1941) represent a culmination of Tolima's literary culture: It is a self-conscious fiction. Each of Sánchez's six early novels is located in a small town in Sánchez's native Tolima. They are accounts of the futility and frustration of life in the *tierra caliente* of Tolima. *Las maniobras* (*The Maneuvers*, 1969) and *Las causas supremas* (*The Supreme Causes*, 1969), his first two novels, demonstrate an explicit self-conscious play with language. The result is a humorous questioning of his own discourse: the narrator always maintains an ironic attitude about language itself. Sánchez's writing is a nihilistic process of constructing and destroying language.

LITERATURE OF GREATER CAUCA

Greater Cauca, centered in the Valle del Cauca, but including Popayán to the south and Chocó to the north, has developed a tradition of cultural heterogeneity. Since the colonial period, Popayán has been a bastion of conventional and elitist literary culture, similar to Bogotá and well-connected with the interior highland and Spain. The Jesuits founded the University of San José in Popayán in 1775. The Valle del Cauca, with Cali as its largest city, has had both the influence of an opulent aristocracy and the populist forces represented by the minority African population and the Antioquian pioneers who settled parts of the Valle del Cauca in the nineteenth and twentieth centuries. The sparsely inhabited Chocó region, geographically and culturally isolated, has been a stronghold of African traditions with relatively little production of literature. Nevertheless, the Afro-Colombian novelist Arnold Palacios (1924) is from Chocó. Chocó was opened to mining in the eighteenth century, even though small settlements were established as early as the sixteenth century, the first being in 1575 in Toro. Popayán was founded in 1535, and Cali in 1536.

The region of greater Cauca has enjoyed a stronger tradition in poetry than greater Tolima, although not as significant as that of the interior highland or greater Antioquia. It is a tradition initiated with the poetry of Jorge Isaacs (1837–1895) and continued with the poetry of Guillermo Valencia (1873–1943), Rafael Maya (1897–1983), Mario Carvajal (1896–1966), Antonio Llanos (born 1905), Gerardo Valencia (born 1911), and Octavio Gamboa (born 1923). Isaacs's poetry represented a minor contribution to Colombian romanticism, whereas Valencia was not only one of greater Cauca's major poets, but a *modernista* poet of national and international recognition. Rafael Maya, originally from Popayán, was an active member of Los Nuevos in Bogotá, as well as one of Colombia's most erudite poetry critics. Maya belonged to the humanist highland-centered tradition of Miguel Antonio Caro, Marco Fidel Suárez, Antonio Gómez Restrepo, and Luis López de Mesa. Mario Carvajal published a book of sonnets of mystical orientation, *La escala de Jacob* (*Jacob's Ladder*, 1935), and three other books of traditional poetry. Gerardo Valencia of Popayán was a minor poet of the Piedra y Cielo group. Antonio Llanos of Cali was of this group's generation, but was not associated with it, and neither his mystical writing nor his poetry of the sea were in line with the Piedra y Cielo poetry. Octavio Gamboa, whose work has gone relatively unrecognized, has written in the tradition of Carvajal and Llanos and published one book, *Canciones y elegías* (*Songs and Elegies*, 1963).

Poets like Carvajal, Llanos, and Gamboa represent a voice particular to a greater Cauca tradition, apart from the central literary movements of the highlands. The literature in greater Cauca has always had a strong tradition of its own, influenced by an amalgam of cultural and historical forces of oral and written culture, and quite independent from the highlands. Isaacs's *María* (1867), the major Colombian novel of the nineteenth century and a classic novel of Latin American romanticism, is representative of greater Cauca's verbal-ideological complexities, but is predominantly a product of Isaac's participation in an elitist literary culture. His family belonged to the Valle del Cauca's upper class, and he associated with Bogotá's intellectuals of *El mosaico* in the 1860s before writing *María* from 1864 to 1866, isolated in the mountains back in the Valle del Cauca. The result was an impressively well-written love story set in the lush Valle del Cauca of Isaacs's childhood. The basic narrative situation is as follows: An adult narrator relates in retrospective fashion the story of his adolescent love affair with María. The narrative is a chronological reconstruction of the events and feelings of the moment. A dedication to "Efraín's brothers" suggests that an unidentified editor made the text on the basis of Efraín's memoirs. There are a few deviations from Isaacs's basic method. These variations appear in the form of interruptions in which the narrator reacts to these past events in the emotional framework of the present. In addition, there is a variation in the narrator's distance from the fictional world he describes: Through the greater part of the novel he reacts intimately to the natural world to which he belongs; during the return trip he describes a new land with more distance.

María is an impressively well-conceived and well-written novel, not only for its period in the context of greater Cauca, but even in a Latin American context. This fact speaks well for the development of literary culture in greater Cauca. This novel was a product of a literary culture for consumption, generally speaking, by the same elite that produced it. Popular literary culture was also present in greater Cauca during the turn of the twentieth century and it had its roots in oral tradition. The creators of this popular literature were poets who were by definition "minor," such as Pedro Antonio Uribe (1854–1934). Uribe's simple verses and sonnets were written for popular consumption on the street corners of Tuluá, a small town in the Valle del Cauca, north of Cali. Uninterested in the classic themes of much literary culture, Uribe wrote a light verse concerned with the topics of daily life in Tuluá and nearby towns. His poems often functioned as newspapers, related orally for an illiterate populace. Consequently, they constitute an unofficial oral history of the region, published posthumously as *Los juglares de Tuluá: Don Pedro Uribe* (*The Tuluá Minstrels: Don Pedro Uribe*, 1984).

The oral tradition of Uribe and the popular vision communicated by its frequent use of *dizque* ("it is said") are integral elements of the fiction of greater Cauca's major twentieth-century writer, Gustavo Alvarez Gardeazábal (born

1945). Alvarez Gardeazábal has, in fact, written of his indebtedness to Uribe. In addition, Alvarez Gardeazábal began writing after the publication of García Márquez's novel of the coastal oral tradition, *One Hundred Years of Solitude*, which had exercised an enormous influence on all literary production in Colombia since 1967.

Alvarez Gardeazábal's first four novels were deeply rooted in the history and oral tradition of the Valle del Cauca, primarily of Tuluá. His first two novels, *La tara del papa* (*The Pope's Defect*, 1971) and *Cóndores no entierran todos los días* (*Condors Don't Bury Everyday*, 1972), are set within the historical context of La Violencia in the Valle del Cauca. *Cóndores no entierran todos los días* relates the story of a local *caudillo* (local chief) who terrorized the Tuluá region during La Violencia, León María Lozano. Both the author's and the narrator's source of information for this story is popular knowledge—the rumor and history that were the essence of Pedro Uribe's poetry. The popular vision of the individual living in a small town is also the primary generator of the anecdotes in *Dabeiba*, a well-elaborated story of a disaster in this town. In *El bazar de los idiotas* (*The Idiots' Bazaar*, 1974), Alvarez Gardeazábal relies on a parody of languages for humorous and critical effects. The parodied language involves García Márquez's *One Hundred Years of Solitude*, the speech of Tuluá's inhabitants, and the official language of the Catholic Church.

In the 1980s and 1990s, Alvarez Gardeazábal has been increasingly involved in politics, following the Colombian (and Latin American) tradition of the man of letters who is active in national politics. His novels of the 1980s were also quite political, in some cases ridiculing known political figures. In 1998, Alvarez Gardeazábal was elected governor of the department of Valle del Cauca, following in the footsteps of such prominent Colombian writer-politicians as Miguel Antonio Caro, Alfonso López Michelsen, and Belisario Betancur.

MODERN LITERATURE

By the mid–1960s, it had become increasingly problematic to read Colombian literature within a strictly regional or even national context. Modern and postmodern writers in Colombia were fully immersed in international literature and film. Most of the communication barriers of the previous century had been overcome by the 1950s, debilitating regional cultures and strengthening Colombia as one society and one culture. Similarly, the magazine *Mito* was modern rather than regional in conception, and national and international in vision. It published writers from all regions of Colombia, including a young Gabriel García Márquez from the Caribbean coast. In addition to the influences of *Mito*, the publication of three Faulknerian novels of very high quality signaled the rise of the modern novel in Colombia: García Márquez's *Leafstorm* (1955), Alvaro Cepeda Samudio's *La casa grande* (1962), and Héctor Rojas Herazo's *Respirando el verano* (1962).

Likewise, the irreverent *nadaístas* of the 1960s contributed to the creation of a more liberal literary atmosphere, conducive to the ongoing production of modern works and further experimentation. These writers—primarily poets—scandalized the still predominantly conservative and conventional cultural establishment. Whether or not the poetry and proclamations of Gonzalo Arango and his *nadaísta* cohorts will be judged of permanent value remains to be seen. Nevertheless, their rebellious textual and extratextual postures had a profound impact on literary tastes and paved the way for ongoing modern and postmodern literary activity in Colombia. The *nadaísta* novel prize (of the 1960s) provided an outlet for the publication and distribution of the most experimental fiction of the time, even though the national concern for understanding and evaluating La Violencia meant that the novel of La Violencia was deemed much more important than novels of technical experimentation.

The literary establishment also provided a heretofore unknown infrastructure for the creation and publication of a national novel of international impact. The magazine *Eco*, published in Bogotá from the early 1960s to the mid–1980s, was essentially European in content, with occasional contributions from Latin America and Colombia. The publishing house Tercer Mundo Editores, which began in the early 1960s, became the first truly national publisher to operate with professional criteria for the publication and national distribution of literature. By the mid-1970s the Editorial Plaza y Janés, a multinational commercial operation based in Spain, was successfully publishing and distributing several Colombian novelists, including Gabriel García Márquez and Gustavo Alvarez Gardeazábal. In the 1980s, a publishing boom in Colombia resulted in the publication of novelists with Plaza y Janés, Tercer Mundo, Planeta, and other firms.

Besides García Márquez, several Colombian writers have successfully assimilated the stratagems of modern fiction, among them Fanny Buitrago, Manuel Zapata Olivella, and Héctor Rojas Herazo. In addition to her short fiction, Buitrago has published several novels in the 1960s, 1970s, and 1980s that emanate from both Caribbean and popular cultures. Zapata Olivella has published six novels, including his most ambitious work, *Changó, el gran putas* (*Chango, the Big S.O.B.*, 1983). This massive novel (more than five hundred pages) is broad in scope, both in terms of history and geography, spanning three continents and six centuries of African and Afro-American history. It begins in Africa and then moves to Colombia and other regions of the Americas, ending in the United States. Héctor Rojas Herazo uses the narrative strategies of a Faulknerian modernity in his trilogy, *Respirando el verano* (*Breathing the Summer*, 1962), *En noviembre llega el arzobispo* (*The Archbishop Arrives in November*, 1967), and *Celia se pudre* (*Celia Is Rotting*, 1986). These novels also evoke the premodern, oral world of Celia, the central character of this trilogy, and her family. *Respirando el verano* focuses on the aging matriarch and her grandson, Anselmo. Celia is a minor character in *En noviembre llega el arzobispo*, a denunciation of the local oligarchy's absolute domination of all sectors of society in the town of Cedrón. It carries with it, in addition, a consistent subtext of terror and violence. *En noviembre llega el arzobispo* characterizes a broader spectrum of society than did the first novel, its social critique being more strident than that of *Respirando el verano*. *Celia se pudre* is Rojas Herazo's lengthy (811-page) summa of the world of Cedrón. Although this hermetic work has multiple narrative voices, the decadence of Cedrón is filtered primarily through Celia's memory. In all three novels, a tone of hatred permeates Cedrón, as well as Celia's life.

Younger writers who have produced a modern fiction since the appearance in 1967 of García Márquez's *One Hundred Years of Solitude* include Gustavo Alvarez Gardeazábal, Héctor Sánchez, Jorge Eliécer Pardo, Germán Espinosa, David Sánchez Juliao, Fernando Vallejo, and Oscar Collazos. Since the late 1970s, the ideological function of Alvarez Gardeazábal's fiction has been unequivocal: it is dedicated primarily to questioning and denouncing greater Cauca's oligarchy. Héctor Sánchez's fiction expresses frustration over the seemingly useless life of its characters, who play out repetitive variations of their tedious daily activity. Germán Espinosa has published several novels of historical impulse, the most accomplished and technically complex of which is *La tejedora de coronas* (*The Weaver of Crowns*, 1982), which takes place during the colonial period. It consists of an interior monologue, a life story related by Genoveva Alcocer, a one hundred-year-old woman accused of witchcraft. David Sánchez Juliao has explored the possibilities of secondary orality (orality of technology), writing a popular fiction using the technology of records and cassettes. Sánchez Juliao embellishes *Pero sigo siendo el rey* (1983) with Mexican *rancheras* and other forms of popular music in order to narrate his melodramatic story of romance and conflict, an anecdote worthy of a soap opera. Fernando Vallejo published the first Colombian novels to deal explicitly with homosexuality, *Los días azules* (*Blue Days*, 1985) and *El fuego secreto* (*The Secret Fire*, 1986). Oscar Collazos published a politically aggressive set of novels, testimonial in impulse, questioning the authority of the Colombian oligarchy and its values.

There are many more modern novelists in Colombia—far too many to mention in an introduction to Colombian literature. A particularly interesting case is the poet Alvaro Mutis. In his poetry, he made references to a fictional character named Maqroll el Gaviero. In the 1980s and 1990s, Mutis published an entire series of novels with Maqroll el Gaviero—sailor, adventurer, and philosopher—as his protagonist. Mutis uses conventional approaches to writing, but his stories have been well received and widely read in Colombia and the remainder of Latin America.

Women writers of the Mutis and García Márquez generation are Flor Romero de Nohra, Rocío Vélez de Piedrahita, and María Helena Uribe de Estrada. This generation of women writers in Colombia, who have not been engaged in the self-conscious and theoretically based feminist discourse of postmodern feminists such as Albalucía Angel, have been relatively conventional in their approach to storytelling. Fanny Buitrago is another productive woman novelist of Angel's generation.

The international recognition attained by García Márquez and the generation of writers he exemplifies, constitutes one literary trend in Colombia—that of modernist fiction. Another, lesser known, trend can be seen in the postmodern gesture of R. H. Moreno-Durán, whose public image as the writer's writer and hermetic exercises gained him the attention of a smaller group of readers, writers, and critics interested in innovative fiction. Solipsistic experiments do not usually become bestsellers, either in the original version or in translation. Nevertheless, Moreno-Durán and writers such as Albalucía Angel, Marco Tulio Aguilera Garramuño, Darío Jaramillo Agudelo, Andrés Caicedo, Rodrigo Parra Sandoval, and Alberto Duque López did pursue an innovative, fundamentally postmodern project during the 1970s and 1980s. Cosmopolitan in interests, most of them have preferred to write abroad; Moreno-Durán and Angel have lived for most of their writing careers in Europe and have been as intellectually attuned to contemporary European writing and theory as to Colombia. Similarly, Duque López has been indelibly influenced by such diverse texts as Julio Cortázar's *Hopscotch* and American film. Aguilera Garramuño has postmodern texts in the sense that they present no privileged narrator upon whom the reader can rely, nor is there an authoritative discourse or figure to whom the reader can turn for something like an objective, final truth regarding its fiction.

The most productive postmodern novelists to date in Colombia have been Moreno-Durán and Angel. The roots of Moreno-Durán's trilogy titled *Fémina Suite (Feminine Suite)* are not found in the empirical reality of Colombia but rather, as in the case of postmodern fiction, in modernist literature. Poems by T. S. Eliot and Paul Valéry generated the first novel of the trilogy, *Juego de damas (Women's Game*, 1977). This novel deals with female intellectuals, beginning with their radicalized student life in the 1960s, and passing through three stages of social climbing and power acquisition. In this novel and the entire trilogy, Moreno-Durán explores the relationships between language and power. Angel's *Misiá Señora* (*Ms. Lady*, 1982) and *Las andariegas* (*The Travelers*, 1984) are part of a feminist project that emanates directly from feminist theory and fiction. She had already published two early experimental novels in the 1970s. Since then, Angel has become the most prominent feminist writer among Colombian novelists, and is recognized by scholars and critics throughout the Americas.

At the turn of the century, both modern and postmodern tendencies are evident in Colombia. In the 1990s, the first generation of writers born in Colombia's television age (since 1955) have begun to publish. Two of the most talented and promising are Philip Potdevin and Octavio Escobar Giraldo. These accomplished novelists draw from literary and historical sources, as well as from television and film.

7

Gabriel García Márquez: The Writer and the Man

Nobel Laureate Gabriel García Márquez has dedicated a lifetime to writing fiction and journalism, beginning in the late 1940s. By the 1990s, he had published more than ten books of fiction and journalistic writings on a regular basis for fifty years. In the process, he has become not only the major writer in the history of Colombia and one of Latin America's central figures of the twentieth century, but also a celebrity figure throughout the Hispanic world. In addition to his exceptional imagination (a trademark of his fiction), he has been a lively and irreverent public intellectual in Latin America, offering comments to the media spiced with the humor, irreverence, and extraordinary intuitive insight that have made him a journalist's dream for the few who have been fortunate enough to interview him.

Upon receiving the Nobel Prize for Literature in 1982, García Márquez was received by President Belisario Betancur, who welcomed him back to his homeland as a hero. Finally he had received the accolades from a nation that had often ignored and sometimes rejected him. His early writings were relatively ignored in Colombia, and his success in the 1960s and 1970s was due much more to the overwhelmingly enthusiastic response of readers, critics, and scholars in Latin America, Europe, and the United States. This enthusiasm was centered primarily on his most accomplished and widely read novel, *One Hundred Years of Solitude*, which appeared in Spanish in 1967 and in English translation in 1970.

García Márquez claims that he had learned everything important in life by the time he was eight. This comment, and his life in itself, point to the fact that this enigmatic figure has always been something of an anomaly in Colombia. A *costeño* with a modest family background, he is a special case as an intellectual giant in a nation where literary culture has been dominated historically by conservative and elite men of letters belonging to Colombia's upper-middle and upper classes. Born in Aracataca in the Caribbean coastal region in 1927, he was an anomaly in Colombia by being the only noteworthy Colombian novelist to have lived in a region dominated by foreign capitalists. Unlike certain Central American and Caribbean nations, Colombia's economy has always been controlled primarily by Colombian nationals, so there have not been any historical "neocolonial" economic powers in Colombia. The one exception to this generalization was the Caribbean coastal region, which was dominated by the United Fruit Company from approximately 1900 to 1928. It departed in 1928, but the young Gabriel García Márquez saw many of the remnants and heard many of the tales of when the *gringos* were in Colombia. He also heard of the 1928 striking banana workers, a situation that resulted in approximately two thousand workers being massacred by government troops. García Márquez's lifetime commitment to leftist politics certainly has much to do with having been reared in an impoverished region in the wake of the United Fruit Company legacy.

Yet another of García Márquez's anomalies is his literary approach to the civil war of La Violencia of the 1950s. The vast majority of Colombian writers during that time wrote blow-by-blow descriptive accounts of the cruelty of this conflict, with lengthy, detailed descriptions of human carnage. In the 1950s, García Márquez was the one Colombian writer who found a totally different approach: He eschewed realist description of blood and violence, and attempted to capture the essence of human relations and human behavior during that period. His subtle and suggestive stories compiled in *Los funerales de la mamá grande* (*Big Mama's Funeral*, these stories appeared under several titles in English) were so indirect in their treatment of politics and violence, in fact, that only the well-informed reader would fully understand the political framework surrounding the characters' thoughts and actions.

García Márquez is unusual in his profound and lifelong commitment to being a professional fiction writer, and a writer only. Most Colombians with the education, talent, and opportunity to publish creative writing have done so as a means to enter the public sphere of politics or the administration of "culture" (such as directing libraries or administering government-funded cultural institutions). Before García Márquez, writing in itself had never been considered a viable "profession" per se. Nevertheless, García Márquez decided early in his life to make his living as a writer, and he has done so by writing first as a professional journalist (from the late 1940s until today), second as a writer of film scripts (in the early 1960s), and finally as a novelist (he has been able to live quite comfortably from novel royalties since 1967). During this entire career—from the late 1940s to the late 1990s—however, García Márquez has been unswerving in his commitment to first becoming and then remaining a fiction writer: Over the past five decades, he has always been planning, writing, or rewriting a piece of fiction. And although he has frequently been willing to take political positions in his role as a public intellectual in Latin America, and occasionally serve as advisor or mediator for Fidel Castro or other Latin American heads of state, García Márquez has remained faithful to his boyhood dream of becoming a writer. Unlike the vast majority of Colombia's prominent public intellectuals, from Miguel Antonio Caro to Belisario Betancur, he has resisted the temptation of political power and a regular income without writing.

BIOGRAPHICAL INTRODUCTION

García Márquez's perhaps tongue-in-cheek affirmation that he had learned everything important in his life by the age of eight probably holds some truth. He was reared by his grandparents from an early age, and has always spoken of them with great admiration. His father was a man of modest means, who left the young Gabriel in the home and care of his grandparents after accepting a position as a telegrapher in another town in the region. As a child, Gabriel was privy to the oral tales told by his grandmother, who was a master of the traditional art of spinning tales. In this tradition, she told "tall tales" full of hyperbole and the other conventions of the genre. In numerous interviews, García Márquez has spoken of his grandmother's impressive mastery of this art, which left a lifelong impression on García Márquez.

As an adolescent, García Márquez was sent to Bogotá to study in a private high school. After completing his high school education, he enrolled in the National University in Bogotá to study law; during that year at the university, he began writing and publishing his first stories (1947). Soon thereafter, with the outbreak of La Violencia, García Márquez moved to the more peaceful Cartagena on the Caribbean coast. In Cartagena and Barranquilla in the late 1940s and early 1950s, García Márquez eked out a minimal existence as a journalist at the same time that he continued writing short fiction and early drafts of a novel that eventually became *Leafstorm* (1955). During these years, his friends were the painter Alejandro Obregón, and the journalists Germán Vargas and Alfonso Fuenmayor, later identified with García Márquez as the "Group of Barranquilla." They read the modern masters who were the models, indeed, the icons for García Márquez and the writers of his generation: Faulkner, Kafka, Hemingway, and Jorge Luis Borges, among others. Although these modernists were his idols, García Márquez also read Western classics thoroughly, from the classical Greeks to Cervantes and Swift.

García Márquez's affinities with Faulkner were numerous, but the Colombian became particularly interested in creating a "total" fictional world around a group of characters in an identifiable region. Thus, Faulkner's fictionalized Oxford County ("Yoknapatawpha County") became García Márquez's fictionalized Aracataca ("Macondo"). With his first novel, *Leafstorm*, he began constructing the world of Macondo, and he followed through with the same setting and many of the same characters in *Big Mama's Funeral*, *No One Writes to the Colonel*, and *In Evil Hour*.

An early turning point for the young aspiring writer was the discovery of Kafka's *Metamorphosis*. Once he read the opening page of that impressive exercise in the fantastic—in which the protagonist awakens one morning to discover that he is no longer a human being but a beetle—García Márquez was awestruck. He claims that it was then, upon discovering Kafka's power of invention, that he decided to become a writer. The reading of Borges gave García Márquez a similar type of inspiration and confidence. There is no doubt that Faulkner, Kafka, and Borges were extremely important, in fact, the key masters, in the formation of the fully accomplished García Márquez of decades later.

In general, the 1950s were difficult, hard-luck years for García Márquez, both in terms of his survival as a writer and his minimal economic survival as a person. In 1955, he went to Paris as a reporter for *El Espectador*, but the military dictator Rojas Pinilla shut the newspaper down, leaving García Márquez unemployed. He remained there for three years—living on a minimal subsistence level and writing the stories that would eventually be published as part of his cycle of Macondo. After returning to Colombia in 1958 and marrying his girlfriend, Mercedes Barcha, he continued working as a journalist in Colombia, Venezuela, and New York, including a brief stint for the Cuban press. This connection with Cuba resulted in García Márquez being placed on a "black list" in the American State Department, making his acquisition of a simple tourist visa to the United States a problematic bureaucratic process.

In the early 1960s, García Márquez traveled from New York to Mexico on a bus, stopping in Oxford, Mississippi to pay homage to his idol, William Faulkner. Once in Mexico, he began working on film scripts, and one of his early projects brought him into contact with Mexican writer Carlos Fuentes, with whom he has since remained a close friend. García Márquez and his wife settled into Mexico City, where they have maintained their principal residence, with occasional stints in Colombia, and with frequent visits to Europe and Cuba.

The turning point in García Márquez's life and career began in the mid–1960s with what was apparently just a typical family vacation from Mexico City to Acapulco. Once the family was on the highway, however, the Colombian author had a kind of revelation or epiphany. Thinking about his writing career, he suddenly realized two important things: first, that he still had one more novel to write, one which would tell the complete story of Macondo, the story he had told only in pieces in his first three books of fiction; and second, that he needed to tell this story the way his grandmother had told him stories, using the conventions of the oral tradition. With this epiphany, he declared the family vacation over, turned back to Mexico City, and went into the basement of his home to write for a year. His wife took care of the family while Gabriel went into virtual isolation. At the end of the year, he had finished his total story of Macondo, *One Hundred Years of Solitude*. Almost just as suddenly, García Márquez became a celebrity writer of the "Boom" of the Latin American novel. In 1967, he participated in an international conference in Caracas with Carlos Fuentes and the new Peruvian star writer, Mario Vargas Llosa. *One Hundred Years of Solitude* immediately sold edition after edition in Spanish, and within three years the same phenomenon happened with the translations. Never before had a single Latin American novel drawn so much attention.

During these glory years of the "Boom," the late 1960s, García Márquez lived in Barcelona, meeting often with his new friend, Mario Vargas Llosa. He was also in regular contact with Fuentes and the fourth member of the Boom, the Argentine Julio Cortázar. These were the years in which García Márquez and the other writers of the Boom consolidated their reputations as being among the most capable writers in the international scenario. García Márquez was living in the wake of the enormous success of *One Hundred Years of Solitude*. Unfortunately, personal and political differences led to an increasing distance among the writers of the Boom in the early 1970s. Differences over support or nonsupport for Fidel Castro's Cuba were the primary reasons for their quarrels.

The last time García Márquez and the other writers of the Boom were together, in fact, was in 1970 in France. A theater festival in Avignon (that included Fuentes's play *El tuerto es rey* [*The One-eyed Man Is King*]) brought them together. Julio Cortázar owned a home near Avignon, in the town of Saignon; Fuentes, García Márquez, Vargas Llosa, and Donoso, along with Spanish writer Juan Goytisolo, met there. The six writers were making plans for a quarterly magazine, *Libre*. Goytisolo was the editor of the journal, which they thought would bring them together, but the effect was the opposite. The arrest of Cuban poet Heberto Padilla had divided Latin American intellectuals, and this affair produced doubts and mistrust among the writers of the Boom. Goytisolo had agreed to serve as editor of the magazine, and intended to publish it as an organ that would support the Cuban regime from the outside and also strengthen the position of intellectuals who, like Padilla, were struggling from the inside for freedom of expression. But *Libre* soon resulted in further divisions among the writers of the Boom and, since then, the friendships and alliances among Latin American writers have been defined, to a large extent, by positions in favor of or against the Cuban government.

In the 1970s, García Márquez was admired by intellectual leftists in Colombia, but generally criticized and rejected by the Colombian citizenry at large. Citizens supporting the two traditional parties tended to view García Márquez as too revolutionary and even "unpatriotic." He supported and financed the leftist political magazine *Alternativa* in Colombia, which supported radical change in the Colombian political and economic system. And despite increasing critiques of Fidel Castro among Latin American intellectuals, García Márquez maintained his personal friendship with Castro and support for the Cuban regime.

Since the 1970s, García Márquez has continued writing fiction and journalism. He has remained a celebrity figure throughout Latin America, but protects his privacy and his right to write with great care. He maintains a small group of close personal friends, which included Germán Vargas and Alejandro Obregón of the former "Group of Barranquilla" until their deaths in the 1990s. He has carefully guarded a close friendship with Fuentes, whom he tends to see with regularity in Mexico City, where they both own homes.

García Márquez has residences in Mexico City, Cartagena (Colombia), Barcelona, and Paris. Living in Colombia has always been problematic for him, both because of his celebrity status and because of security issues in Colombia.[1] Since 1982, nevertheless, he has returned to Colombia with regularity, spending anywhere from a few days to several months there, usually in Cartagena and Bogotá. He often visits Cuba, where he has offered film script writing workshops to young Cubans.

With rare exceptions, García Márquez has avoided the lecture circuit and ignored scholars and critics interested in his work. His primary reason for accepting virtually none of the thousands of annual invitations to deliver lectures and/or receive awards is his dislike of public speaking and a commitment to his writing. His distance from scholars and critics is due primarily to his long-standing distrust of the critical enterprise, although in recent years his attitude has changed slightly.[2]

Despite García Márquez's lifelong critique of many of Colombia's most revered institutions (the Catholic Church; the traditional political parties), he has maintained friendships with members of a generation involved in the institutionalized politics. For example, García Márquez was a very close friend of

Belisario Betancur, president of Colombia, 1982–1986

former president Belisario Betancur during his presidency (1982–1986) and has always had good personal relations with former president Alfonso López Michelsen. Both of these political figures, of course, are intellectuals in their own right. During the presidency of liberal César Gaviria (1990–1994), García Márquez was in constant contact with the president, frequently offering advice and consultation.

INTRODUCTION TO THE FICTION OF GARCÍA MÁRQUEZ

Since the 1960s, the name of Gabriel García Márquez has been virtually synonymous with the term "magic realism." Indeed, the masterful juxtaposition of the magical and the everyday in *One Hundred Years of Solitude* made this novel a modern classic of Latin American magic realism.[3] García Márquez, however, claims that he is a realist who merely describes Colombian reality.

Not all of García Márquez's work has been written in the magic realist vein; his career as a fiction writer can be divided into three distinct periods: The first (1947–1954), consisted of his initial short stories, which had little or nothing to do with magic realism; the second (1955–1967) is his cycle of fiction set in Macondo, some of which does contain magic realist elements; and the third

(1968–present) is his post–Macondo work, most of which involves new directions for García Márquez, beyond magic realism.

García Márquez's fiction published from 1947 to 1954 marked a period from his first inventions to the establishment of his professional identity as a writer by the mid–1950s. These first stories were more important as initial explorations and a symbolic beginning than for their artistic merit. In his very first story, "La tercera resignación" ("The Third Resignation"), he attempts to create a literature like Kafka—a fiction that defies the rational limits of what is normally accepted as everyday empirical reality. This story deals with a man who is apparently dead, but who seems to function in some gray area between the normal categories of life and death. The story's initial frame of reference is totally interior, psychological. At the outset, the exact circumstances of the protagonist are ambiguous and even confusing: He suffers from something which the reader is not able to clarify in the first three paragraphs. In the third paragraph, the ambiguity becomes a frontal attack on our rational sense of the reality of the story, for the narrator points out that the protagonist had already died once before. The remainder of the story elaborates on this peculiar state, which the narrator identifies as a "living death." In this story, García Márquez is overtly preoccupied with the creation of some kind of "other reality" along the lines of what he had recently discovered in his readings of Kafka and other modern masters.

The remainder of the stories written during this early period share several of the characteristics, accomplishments, and defects of his first story. They reveal a writer experimenting with the potentiality of different points of view. "La otra costilla de la muerte" ("The Other Side of Death") represents another overt attempt to create "another reality," but with a different approach from the first story. It deals with a man who seems to suffer from insomnia after the death of his twin brother. The beginning places the reader in the unstable oneiric world of the first story. After a series of surrealistic, shocking images at the beginning of the story, the man realizes that he is terrorized by the image of his brother suffering the agony of death. For the first time, he thinks about the heredity which links him with his brother and, more surprisingly, the possibility that part of his own self could find itself dead with his brother. He concludes that he will eventually rot with his brother. At first such a thought horrifies him, but he gradually becomes attracted to the simplicity of death, until at the end of the story he resigns himself to it.

The intercalation of interior monologues within the third-person narration in this story creates a closeness to the oneiric and terrifying effects of the situation for the reader. The use of the two narrators also maintains the sensation of confusion established in the opening section of the story. In addition, this alteration of narrative point of view emphasizes the conflict between exterior reality, described in third person, and the interior, psychological reality of first person.

The portrayal of an absurd and irrational world is also both the goal and effect of one of the longest of these early stories, "Eva está dentro de su gato" ("Eva Is Inside Her Cat"). Indeed, it is essentially the same story communicated in the two previous ones, with a change in character. This character, Eva, lives in a world in which all "dimensions" have been eliminated. It is a type of limbo that seems to be in touch with both the "real" world and another world in death. She remembers that spirits can be reincarnated in living bodies, and decides to be reborn in her cat. At this point, the story takes yet another step toward the fantastic within the realm of the fantastic: She discovers that neither the cat nor her house exists any longer, for three thousand years have passed since she lived in the world of life. As in all fantastic literature, of course, this series of events, as well as her state of existence, is inexplicable.

"Diálogo del espejo" ("Dialogue with the Mirror") and "Tubal-Caín forja una estrella" ("Tubal-Caín Forges a Star") are exercises in modernist literature par excellence. They function on the basis of different schemes. The scheme of the latter uses free association as its structural device. It is an incoherent and relatively ineffective story. The former deals with a businessman who arises and prepares himself for a day at the office. His sense of pettiness and monotony is typical of the literature of the ennui of modern life. It uses as its point of departure a real-world setting and then exploits another level of reality through the doubling effect the protagonist experiences observing himself in the bathroom mirror. The apparent incoherence and unconnected ideas in this story make it a classic piece of youthful experimentation with language.

A first-person narrator in "Alguien desordena estas rosas" ("Someone Has Been Disarranging These Roses"), in contrast, serves as the basis for one of the most successful of these early stories. The special nature of the situation, the fact that the narrator is dead, is established in the story's first line. Apart from this fact, which the reader accepts from the beginning, the story functions in a real world, in contrast to the fantastic nature of the other stories. This dead voice that announces in the first line that it will carry a bouquet of flowers to the tomb is in fact the voice of a little boy who had died forty years before, falling down a staircase. For the past twenty years, he has lived with the woman who had been his faithful childhood friend. The house has a small chapel, and each Sunday a breeze places the flowers on this altar in disarray. In reality, the cause of the disheveled flowers is the spirit of this boy, who each Sunday tries in vain to take a bouquet of roses from the house to his own tomb. This story seems to resemble the fables of ambulatory ghosts of the sort that García Márquez heard from his grandparents in that house supposedly full of ghosts. Indeed, this story represents a notable transition from the horror-fantasy of those first stories to what would later be the literature of Macondo. Published in 1952, it is more Faulknerian in tone and technique than the initial stories from the late 1940s. The use of a first-person narrator as a technical device to create suspense is quite likely a lesson learned from the reading of Faulkner. This story belongs to the period when García Márquez's fiction of Macondo was beginning to take form. This story, which uses the special ambience of a home as the base, corresponds strikingly to the situation in *Leafstorm*, the novel that officially initiates the cycle of Macondo. Both the rough draft for *Leafstorm* and this story were written in the early 1950s.

An initial perusal of these early García Márquez stories virtually precludes relating them to the inventor of Macondo. Some scholars have affirmed that a reading of these stories makes it difficult to believe that they were first steps in his literary career. Their overt experimentation with universal experience and sense of play with reality itself, however, point to a writer conscientiously creating something for consumption beyond narrow national boundaries.

García Márquez published two short stories in 1955, and they demonstrate radical changes from the stories of the adolescent writer. Most important within the context of the Colombian's total writing career is the invention of Macondo. This marvelous town provides a clearly defined Latin American geographical setting, rather than the abstract spaces of the first stories. Macondo would be further defined and invented for some ten years.

"Monologue of Isabel Watching It Rain in Macondo" is a first-person narration which tells the story of Macondo's being inundated by rain. Given the constant presence of rain in García Márquez's later fiction (it will be important in *No One Writes to the Colonel*), it is perhaps appropriate that the first paragraph of the first story about Macondo deals with rain. The monologue covers five days, Sunday through Thursday, a period during which the situation in Macondo, due to the rains, becomes progressively worse. The narrator-protagonist's perception of the general situation and her own particular circumstance make the story more than just a tale about a town's confrontation with a physical disaster.

The story begins with the rain; from the moment the townfolk leave church, they run to find cover from the cloudburst. Isabel finds the new water refreshing at first, and her father interprets it as a sign that there will be ample water for a year. As the rain continues, the narrator contemplates the past, hot days of August before the rains. She, like the remainder of the family, watches the rain in boredom as she also awaits the birth of a son. By Tuesday a cow appears, and the Indians are ordered to scare it off; they do not succeed. The continuous flow of the rain seems to affect and even pain the protagonist. The family grows numbed and insensitive from the rain, as its monotony wears on them. They reach a point by Thursday at which their only functional sense is that of touch. The end of the story contains a final surprise: both the narrator and the reader discover that she, in fact, is dead.

The details of the development of this story reveal a series of subtle changes that reflect the progressive deterioration of the family. In fact, the entire story is a process of breaking down any sense of homogeneous unity. The first change—the weather—seems insignificant initially, but is part of a larger process of literal transformation of the physical world. The physical environment, in turn, has effects on the mental state of the characters. There is also a change in everyday life; a breakdown in rational order. For example, the characters lose track of the most regular of all daily routines, the order of meals, and the narrator even states that from that moment on they quit thinking.

The final step in this bizarre series of changes in the physical and mental world of the protagonist occurs on Thursday. On one hand, the protagonist loses all sense of time and place. The physical world has been transformed in such a way that even human bodies are "improbable." The end of the story resolves an ambiguous situation. The surprising revelation that the protagonist is dead makes the flexibility of the physical world at least understandable. It is the final step in the creation of a physical world that escapes rational explanation.

"Monologue of Isabel Watching It Rain in Macondo" is a transition between the initial stories of the 1947–1954 period and the later magic realist fiction of Macondo. As in the initial stories, García Márquez is clearly interested in placing into question traditional concepts of time and space, and tends to privilege the use of the language of "time" as part of his discourse. The progressive flow of rain eventually creates that "other reality" to which García Márquez also aspired in the earlier stories. Once again, this is a special kind of inexplicable stage between life and death, and this story makes a significant beginning because it is the first story of Macondo.

"Tale of a Castaway" belongs to a genre located somewhere in the realm of creative journalism, or journalistic fiction. Some critics mention the story briefly with reference to García Márquez's writing; rarely is it included as an integral part of his short fiction. This oversight is paradoxical because of the recognized fact that the development of García Márquez's writing is closely tied to his journalistic career.

The "Tale of a Castaway" was published originally as fourteen serialized articles in Bogotá's newspaper, *El Espectador*. It reconstructed the story of a real person, Luis Alejandro Velasco, a twenty-year-old sailor who was shipwrecked while aboard the Colombian ship *Caldas* in February 1955. García Márquez interviewed him extensively to acquire his basic anecdotal material; the result was a superb adventure story. The fourteen anecdotes tell Velasco's story from his last days in Mobile, Alabama, before the ship's departure, through the ten days he spent on a raft, and, at the end, his reception in Colombia as a hero.

Seen within the context of García Márquez's total fiction, the story is notably his and not really Velasco's. The writer uses Velasco's heroic venture as material for articulating one of his constant literary preoccupations, conventional concepts of time and space. As such, Velasco suffers from the type of experience with reality that many of García Márquez's characters from the 1947–1954 period had perceived.

García Márquez's initial discovery of such writers as Kafka, Borges, and Faulkner in the 1940s had inspired a frontal attack on traditional concepts of time and space. His work on *Leafstorm*, actually written in the early 1950s well before this "Tale of a Castaway," reflects a concern for Colombia's concrete historical reality. He obviously felt a need to deal with both abstract and empirical reality. The "Tale of a Castaway" in a certain way freed García Márquez momentarily from this dilemma and concerns about concrete reality in particular: The priority was entertainment. García Márquez used this opportunity just to tell a good story, a skill he continued to use adroitly no matter what the nature of the fictional world or social context.

The first novel of the Macondo cycle was *Leafstorm* (1955). Most of the action in this work takes place in Macondo from 1903 to 1928. The word "action" is slightly misleading, for *Leafstorm* is more a novel of atmosphere than events. Events are blurred by a sequence and lack of explanation that quite often make their rational understanding secondary to their effects. All the characters in "Monologue of Isabel Watching It Rain in Macondo" are present in this novel. Thus, the short story is modified by a reading of this novel, just as this novel is modified by a reading of *One Hundred Years of Solitude*. All of the fiction of Macondo functions in this manner. *Leafstorm* was written in the early 1950s (1951), and "Monologue of Isabel Watching It Rain in Macondo" was a product of the same rough draft that produced the novel.[4]

Leafstorm is the story of Macondo; the focus lies primarily on four characters: three people in a family who narrate, and a doctor whose wake is the basic circumstance of the novel. The work consists of twenty-nine segments, ranging in length from about three to five pages. After an initial segment which is narrated from a collective "we" point of view, the story changes to the first of three narrators in the family, a ten-year-old boy. The boy, at the wake, relates his thoughts and perceptions of the moment. The other voices are the boy's mother, Isabel, and his grandfather.

The most important event to take place in this small town during this quarter century is the arrival and departure of the "leafstorm"—the people and unbridled progress associated with an American banana company. The once innocent and rural town becomes a center for the chaos and corruption often linked with nascent modernity. The "banana boom" results in a swift but artificial prosperity that produces scenes in which money is burned in celebrations. The nouveau riche of the teens, along with the workers that follow them, are resented by the town's founders. The grandfather, for example, belongs to this group of the older families, the historical aristocracy, that precedes the arrival of the company and resents the anonymous mass of people associated with it.

When asked in 1982 what he thought about the young writer who authored this first novel, García Márquez explained that he views him with "a little compassion, because he wrote it quickly, thinking that he wasn't going to write anything else in this life, that that was his only opportunity, and so he tried to put into that book everything learned by then. Especially techniques and literary tricks taken from American and English novels that he was reading."[5] Even without being aware of García Márquez's direct Faulknerian connection, the techniques most apparently adopted from the modern masters are the use of structure and point of view from Faulkner's *As I Lay Dying*. Concerned with some critics' contention that *Leafstorm* is little more than a Spanish version of this Faulkner novel, García Márquez stated, with the considerable advantage of retrospection, that *Leafstorm* "isn't exactly the same [as *As I Lay Dying*]. I utilize three points of view without giving them names: that of an old man, a boy, and a woman. If you look carefully, *Leafstorm* has the same technique (points of view organized around a dead person) as *The Autumn of the Patriarch*. Only that in *Leafstorm* I didn't dare let myself loose, the monologues are rigorously systematized."[6]

As García Márquez's initial novel-length voyage into the increasingly magical land of Macondo, *Leafstorm* is a remarkably successful venture in the creation of an "other reality." This success is due to the ability to fictionalize a reader who experiences a myth, rather than needing it to be explained. The intricacies of the structure and the characters are a process discovered by the reader, who assumes a necessarily active role in reconstructing a Macondo in a present state of disintegration. Both a specifically Colombian social reality and a universal experience are important of this first novel by García Márquez.

Paradoxically, it was during the period that García Márquez was most distanced from Colombia (in Paris) that he became intimately involved with its specific sociopolitical realities in his fiction. It was during his stay outside Colombia in the middle to late 1950s that he wrote most of the stories later published as *Big Mama's Funeral* and two short novels, *No One Writes to the Colonel* and *In Evil Hour*. In 1970, García Márquez explained his move as follows: "I decided to approach the reality of the moment in Colombia and I wrote *No One Writes to the Colonel* and *In Evil Hour*."[7] Twelve years later he offered a more precise description of the fiction of this period: "*No One Writes to the Colonel* and *Big Mama's Funeral* are books inspired in Colombia's reality and their rationalist structure is determined by the nature of the theme. I don't regret having written them, but they constitute a type of premeditated literature that offers a somewhat static and exclusive view of reality." With these three books, García Márquez fictionalizes the political and human reality of Colombia—its institutions and the effects of its civil war. He also continues to develop some of his already established literary preoccupations and ambitions, including the construction of a broader world of Macondo, with occasional hints of the magic that eventually became his trademark.

With respect to the volume *Big Mama's Funeral* (1962), the first line of the title story brings to García Márquez's fiction a very important element previously lacking in his writing: hyperbolic humor. It begins as follows:

> This is, for all the world's unbelievers, the true account of Big Mama, absolute sovereign of the Kingdom of Macondo, who lived for ninety-two years, and died in the odor of sanctity one Tuesday last September, and whose funeral was attended by the pope.

There is a considerable use of such humor in this story. The volume is not uniformly humorous hyperbole, although it does contain some humor and other elements new to the author's fictional world. In this volume, two stories of this type are "Balthazar's Marvelous Afternoon" and "One Day After Saturday." Some of the stories represent a further development of the literature of Macondo, which involved not only locating the stories there, but also developing characters who would regularly appear in the Macondo fiction. This is one way that García Márquez's fiction is modified by reading: Just as the reader's experience of "Monologue of Isabel Watching It Rain" is changed after reading *Leafstorm*, the experience of *One Hundred Years of Solitude* will be changed after gaining an awareness of these stories. Some of these stories, such as "One of These Days" and "Montiel's Widow," deal with La Violencia.

The volume's title story, "Big Mama's Funeral," as its name and first line suggest, tells the story of the funeral for this most prodigious woman. The narrator explains at the beginning that, now that all the commotion has calmed down, he will tell the true story of the events relating to her funeral, before the historians have time to arrive on the scene. Approximately the first half of the story relates more details concerning the death scene and the immediate surroundings.

In the second half, it is revealed that her death has immediate impact on the entire nation: The newspapers carry her picture as a twenty-year-old and are filled with articles about her illustrious life. Even the pope prepares for the funeral, making a canoe trip to Macondo. He is joined by representatives from all levels of the institutional bureaucracy, even the numerous beauty queens of Colombia's different festivals.

The humor in "Big Mama's Funeral" depends on the success of the hyperbole and the invitation the reader receives to assume an appealing (and superior) role. The reader is invited to play a similarly superior role in the story "Balthazar's Marvelous Afternoon." There, the superiority arises directly in relationship to the story's poor protagonist, Balthazar. In general, the humor in "Balthazar's Marvelous Afternoon" is achieved with more delicate touches than in the overwhelming and raucous hyperbole of "Big Mama's Funeral." The characterization of the protagonist, Balthazar, and his wife, Ursula, as opposites are a matter of light humor, rather than devastating satire.

The third of this trio of stories which share different aspects of humor is "One Day After Saturday." This, an early story of the volume, was awarded a prize in 1955 by the Association of Colombian Artists and Writers. García Márquez uses a technique that will be successfully exploited in his later fiction, such as *In Evil Hour* and "A Very Old Man with Enormous Wings": the entrance of an element foreign to society which interrupts its regular sense of order. The strange element is a growing number of dead birds that seem to be falling into all parts of the town. This odd situation occasions the breakdown of everyday order which provides García Márquez with his point of departure. This use of an inexplicable, irrational element which interrupts the regular sense of order is preparation for the magic realism of *One Hundred Years of Solitude*.

No One Writes to the Colonel is a short novel (ninety-two pages in the Spanish edition) which tells the story of an aged colonel and his life in a small town. The silence of this novel is inscribed by an articulated and also a nonarticulated political censorship. The colonel, as well as Macondo's other inhabitants, avoids political language at all costs. The political situation is the essential and overriding factor in everyone's lives. Consequently, the existence of this minimalized political discourse, resulting in a discourse of silence, is the novel's outstanding feature. The fact that the novel's "present" is the mid–1950s is quite important because it is the period of intense political violence and repression in Colombia—La Violencia. The seventy-five-year-old protagonist was a colonel in the War of a Thousand Days (1899–1902) at the age of twenty. He fought alongside Colonel Buendía, a well-known figure from García Márquez's other books.

The basic setting and situations of this novel present a dismal picture of violence and depravity. Like some of the short stories from this period, however, *No One Writes to the Colonel* also contains humor. The main source of humor, as in "Big Mama's Funeral," is language itself.

The constant but subtle references to the political situation make the book above all about politics. Both generations of the novel's family have been rendered neutral, impotent, by established authority: the ex-revolutionary colonel waits hopelessly for nonexistent financial support; the son has been assassinated because of his supposedly subversive political activity. Despite the dismal political situation, and the portrayal of a people reduced to silence, the total vision presented in the novel is not entirely negative. The firm dignity of certain characters in García Márquez's stories is recalled in the more fragile—but constant—dignity of the colonel. Several scholars, in fact, have referred to the fundamental optimism of this novel. This is an early example of the basic affirmation for humanity found in García Márquez's later work, most notably the masterpiece that would later synthesize all this fiction of Macondo, *One Hundred Years of Solitude*.

In Evil Hour (1962) deals with the same basic sociopolitical context in Colombia (La Violencia), but the presentation is much more direct; violence and other physical acts are visible. Subversion and repression are not the nonarticulated taboo subjects of clandestine newspapers or private conversations, but the central actions of the novel, which tells the story of life in an unnamed town during seventeen days, October 4–21. This unnamed town, of course, is Macondo.

The reader acquainted with García Márquez's earlier books will note that *In Evil Hour* involves a certain synthesizing process that will be intensified later in *One Hundred Years of Solitude*: Several characters and situations from the previous stories appear in *In Evil Hour*. The recognizable characters include Don Sabas, Father Angel, and the mayor from *No One Writes to the Colonel*. Another sign will be displayed that prohibits talk about politics. The dentist from "One of These Days" reappears, again inflicting pain on the mayor. In addition, the reader encounters the Montiel family from "Balthazar's Marvelous Afternoon" and "Montiel's Widow," Mina and Trinidad from "Artificial Roses," and Don Roque from "In This Town There Are No Thieves," among other characters.

In Evil Hour consists of ten unnumbered chapters, a total of forty brief sections, which present a panoramic view of life in the town. The use of these sections and montage techniques make the novel an experience for the reader of organizing a story, rather than following a linear story line, as is offered in *No One Writes to the Colonel*. A certain story, with subplots, does emerge. The characters begin noticing the appearance of lampoons on the streets of Macondo, accusing members of the local oligarchy of scandalous activity. Eventually, the threat of subversion offered by the lampoons is realized with the appearance of a clandestine newspaper. Near the end of the book, political repression increases; dissidents depart to the mountains to join the guerrillas. At the end, the mayor himself admits that the area is in a state of war. The lampoons which had generated the open conflict seem to symbolize resistance to the order imposed upon the town.

The most successful and accomplished of García Márquez's works, *One Hundred Years of Solitude*, is the story of the Buendía family and the story of Macondo. José Arcadio Buendía marries his cousin, Ursula, and they are the illustrious first generation of a prodigious seven-generation family. Because of their kinship, José Arcadio and Ursula, and all of their descendants, fall in love despite the threat and terror of engendering a child with a pig's tail. The novel can also be described as the story of Macondo, which is founded by José Arcadio Buendía. Macondo progresses from a primary village to a modern town, after the arrival of electricity, lights, and other twentieth-century conveniences. It also suffers the vicissitudes of Colombia's history, including its civil wars. This is the synthesis of García Márquez's Macondo cycle and, in many ways, the summa of Colombian literature and history written during the first century and a half of its independence.

One Hundred Years of Solitude is a sophisticated product of literary culture juxtaposed with much of the mind-set of the oral culture of his youth in Aracataca, reinforced in the author's experience by his grandmother. Both oral culture and literary culture permeate *One Hundred Years of Solitude*, often in hilarious juxtaposition. Much of this novel re-creates precisely the shift from orality to writing, changes hitherto labeled as shifts from "magic" to "science," which can be more cogently explained as shifts from orality to various stages of literacy.

This transition is essential to the experience of *One Hundred Years of Solitude* and is particularly evident when one compares the initial chapters with the ending. In the first chapter, the mind-set of a primary orality predominates; in the last, the most intricate exercises of writing culture are carried out. In the beginning, these two extremes are represented by Melquíades of a writing culture from the outside and by Ursula with a mind-set of orality. After the first chapter, Macondo moves from preliteracy to literacy.[8]

Numerous critics have used the term "magic realism" with respect to this novel. The German art critic Franz Roh first coined the term in 1925, as a magic insight into reality. For Roh, it was synonymous with postexpressionist painting (1920–1925) because it revealed the mysterious elements hidden in everyday reality. Magic realism expressed man's astonishment before the wonders of the real world; José Arcadio Buendía's amazement over Melquíades's ice is an indication why the term seems appropriate in a discussion of García Márquez. Nevertheless, what has been identified as magic realism in *One Hundred Years of Solitude* can be more precisely described as the written expression of the multiple effects produced by the interplay between oral and written cultures. In this novel, García Márquez has fictionalized numerous aspects of his youth in the triethnic oral culture of the rural Caribbean coastal region. Its unique traditionalism and modernity are based on the various roles the narrator assumes as oral storyteller in the fashion of the tall tale, as a narrator with an oral person's mind-set, and as the modern narrator of a self-conscious (written) fiction.

In addition to being a synthesis of García Márquez's Macondo cycle, *One Hundred Years of Solitude* represents a culmination of two major tendencies in the novel of the Costa. It is a stunning combination of oral and writing traditions only partially achieved in previous texts published in Colombia. It also represents a synthesis of history that numerous novelists and even more historians have attempted to write in Colombia since the nation's independence.

Since completing the cycle of Macondo, García Márquez has published several other books of fiction that can be considered the third period of his work. Several of his novels have been bestsellers in Latin America and beyond, and all are well-written entertainments; the critical consensus, nevertheless, is that none of these works is as well-wrought and important as *One Hundred Years of Solitude*. Since 1967, García Márquez has published several volumes of short stories and four novels.

With respect to the stories, he has published *The Incredible and Sad Tale of Innocent Erendira and Her Heartless Grandmother* (1972) and *Strange Pilgrims* (1993). Both volumes are, above all, entertainments—the product of a mature writer who obviously takes pleasure in both writing and entertaining. Over the past three decades, García Márquez has been able to enjoy what he does best, writing good stories. Although written in quite different stages of his career, they represent his successful effort to leave Macondo behind and move into new literary terrains.

Since 1967, García Márquez has published the following novels: *The Autumn of the Patriarch* (1975), *Chronicle of a Death Foretold* (1981), *Love in the Times of Cholera* (1985), *The General in His Labyrinth* (1989), and *Of Love and Other Demons* (1994). Some of these novels disappointed those of his readers who associated García Márquez exclusively with the enchantment and magic of Macondo. None of these works returns the reader to Macondo, and the magic realism of *One Hundred Years of Solitude* is less evident.

The Autumn of the Patriarch, in fact, is García Márquez's most difficult book to read, and not surprisingly it has never had a readership as broad as *One Hundred Years of Solitude*. Judged strictly on its own intrinsic artistic merit, however, *The Autumn of the Patriarch* is a major book for both García Márquez and the field of the contemporary Latin American novel. It was one of several Latin American novels appearing in the 1970s dealing with a dictator, who in this case is the protagonist. A more precise definition of the theme, however, is not dictatorship but power. Since the 1950s, García Márquez has been fascinated with the power and personality of Venezuelan dictators Juan Vicente Gómez and Pérez Jiménez. The novel involves a series of anecdotes that relate to the life of a dictator identified as "the general." The anecdotes do not appear in chronological order; in addition, they include such gross anachronisms as the presence of Christopher Columbus and American marines in the same scene.

The maintenance of power in *The Autumn of the Patriarch* is determined by the general's ability to manipulate the visible and the invisible. After a potential assassin fails to kill him, the General not only orders the man put to death, but more significantly in the context of his own understanding of the importance of the visible, he orders that the different parts of the assassin's body be exhibited throughout the country, thus providing a visible manifestation of the consequences of questioning the general's power. The question of the visible and the invisible and its relation to the novel's main theme—power—is also elaborated through the presence of the sea (*mar*) in the novel.

Publication of the brief novel *Chronicle of a Death Foretold* showcased García Márquez the journalist. The journalist-fiction writer penned a story of love and revenge, based on events that had happened to some of García Márquez's best friends of thirty years before. The perennially vague line distinguishing fact and fiction in García Márquez's writing, as well as the line between the journalist and the novelist, was made even more nebulous. The novel consists of five brief chapters which are not exactly a "chronicle" if one holds to the dictionary definition of this genre—a chronological record of historical events. The first chapter recounts the morning of their assassination by the two brothers, who are called Pedro and Pablo Vicario in the novel. The second relates the background of the relationship between future husband and wife, Bayardo San Román and Angela Vicario, and carries the pair's story forward to the evening of the wedding. The third chapter deals with the evening of the wedding, the night before Santiago Nasar's death. There is a temporal move forward in the fourth chapter, which tells of the events subsequent to the tragedy, such as the autopsy of Santiago Nasar and Angela Vicario's life during the years after the failed marriage. The last chapter returns to the chronology of events surrounding the actual assassination, culminating in a detailed and graphic description of the death.

The real-world setting of this work is not Aracataca, but Sucre, another town in the Caribbean coastal region. García Márquez is far from Macondo. Nevertheless, certain touches in *Chronicle of a Death Foretold* evoke the Macondo cycle: dreams and premonitions that are incorrectly interpreted, the ambiguous and flexible distance between the occurrence of events and their reconstruction, and events that seem to carry a symbolic meaning (such as the rains, the insomnia, the dreams, and the odors that are called moral indicators). There would seem to be an underlying system here that provides a profound and coherent understanding of things, but there is not. Rather, as in all of García Márquez's works, life is determined by inexplicable forces and irrational acts.

Since being awarded the Nobel Prize for Literature, all of García Márquez's fiction has been readily available to a vast reading public, and all of his works, including the more recent *Love in the Times of Cholera* (a novel about aging) and *The General in His Labyrinth* (a novel about the historical figure Simón Bolívar) are highly regarded by most professional critics. Nevertheless, the general consensus among scholars and critics is that his literary masterpieces— to be read in future decades as classics of Latin American literature—are *One Hundred Years of Solitude*, *The Autumn of the Patriarch*, and *No One Writes to the Colonel*. These works have made him both a major writer of the Spanish language and the most impressive intellectual figure in the history of Colombia.

8

The Plastic Arts, Photography, and Architecture

The plastic arts, photography and architecture, like Colombian literature, entered into a modern phase in the 1940s and 1950s. In this period, most of the painters and architects aligned themselves with what was called the "international" school. Contemporary Colombian painters and sculptors, such as Fernando Botero, Alejandro Obregón, and Enrique Grau hold international reputations as world-class innovators. Many other Colombian painters, such as Edgar Negret and Omar Rayo, are also recognized throughout Latin America, Europe, and the United States. Colombian photographers and architects, on the other hand, have reached an admirable level of expertise without ever becoming innovators recognized beyond the borders of Colombia.

Generally speaking, the plastic arts and architecture were Spanish productions in the colonial period from the sixteenth to the nineteenth centuries. In the nineteenth century, painting, sculpture, and architecture tended to be imitative of European art and architecture of the period. Twentieth-century art and architecture has been dominated by a desire to be modern. In recent years, some of Colombia's voluminous artistic production and expanding urban space have taken a postmodern turn. Writing in the mid–1980s, Gabriel García Márquez estimated that Colombian painters were a *plaga marvillosa* (marvelous plague) of between a thousand and five thousand painters. When García Márquez made this statement, then President Belisario Betancur supported a project to identify the 130 most accomplished young Colombian painters who were painting and exhibiting abroad. The result was an impressive art show exhibiting a broad range of gifted painters born in the 1950s and 1960s. Their work is clear testimony to the fact that the present and future of Colombian art is bright.

PLASTIC ARTS

Colombian painting has become internationally recognized, and increasingly prominent since the 1960s. Internationally acclaimed painters and sculptors include Botero, Obregón, Grau, Beatriz González, Edgar Negret, Eduardo Ramírez, and Olga de Amaral. Sculpture has been a relatively minor cultural expression, beginning to make its mark in the 1970s, although in several cases the sculpture was produced by artists already well known as painters.

Colombian artists entered into a nationalist and indigenous phase (identified as the "Bachué" movement) in the 1930s under the influence of the new Mexican art that had grown out of the Mexican Revolution. Among these artists, the most prominent was Pedro Nel Gómez (1899–1984), known primarily as a muralist painter dedicated to nationalist and indigenous themes, always in the role of social critic. His murals can be seen on numerous public buildings in Medellín. During the 1930s and 1940s, Gómez was something of an innovator, as were other artists of the same period, such as the drawer Ignacio Gómez Jaramillo and the sculptor Luis Alberto Acuña.

Gómez, Gómez Jaramillo, and Acuña saw themselves as participants in a new "universal" movement in art that was also taking place in architecture. They wanted to be profoundly Latin American and universal in their themes, but soon were considered mere relics of an indigenous art with excessively strong nationalistic overtones. Their work, nevertheless, was basically quite traditional in form and technique. A truly modernist spirit in art, however, surfaced in Colombia in the 1940s and 1950s with the appearance of the painting of Alejandro Obregón, Enrique Grau, Edgar Negret, and Eduardo Ramírez Villamizar. Obregón's painting has always been close to both the figurative and the abstract. An artist from the Caribbean who often associated with García Márquez's "Group of Barranquilla" in the 1940s, Obregón aspired not only to universalize Colombian painting, but also to move it in directions beyond the social message and the nationalism of the previous generation (Pedro Nel Gómez and cohorts). For Obregón and Grau, their predecessors were too direct in the expression of their social concerns and too narrow in their nationalism. In the 1950s, in fact, there was a generalized reaction against the "Bachué" group and the work of Pedro Nel Gómez.

Obregón's abstractions, always with bright colors, seem to evoke the sun, the sea, and the magic of the Caribbean. He has gained a well-deserved reputation as one of the masters in Latin America. His work can be associated with the "magic realism" of the García Márquez generation in literature.

Obregón's work developed in four periods. The first two (1944–1948 and 1949–1954) involved his initial training and a personal search. He reached his maturity as an artist in the third stage (1955–1967), during which he was the

Mural by Alejandro Obregón in Barranquilla

most influential painter in Colombia, using a style that is very particular to Obregón. This style is his own particular brand of expressionism which typically includes the representation of figures such as condors, bulls, and a variety of fish, sea animals, and flora associated with the Caribbean. Obregón's style and themes are quite personal and recognizable as his; in the 1960s, this work brought him broad recognition as a leading painter of the Americas. During his fourth period (from 1968 to the 1990s), Obregón did not have the same impact in the Americas, and his painting was considered less significant in Colombia as well. He continued work along many of the lines already established—using some of the same Caribbean images and colors—but his work lacked the boldness and energy of the 1950s and 1960s.

Grau and Ramírez Villamizar cultivate a broad range of styles and interests, from Grau's occasional use of figurative anecdotes and the intentionally decadent, to the abstract and geometric compositions of Ramírez Villamizar. In the total careers of these two painters, they have used a variety of languages associated with modernist painting in Latin America and beyond. Grau has dedicated much of his painting to human figures, with occasional touches of Renaissance influence. He has allowed some space for humor and entertainment with comical juxtapositions, for example, of the everyday and the unreal that invite comparisons with García Márquez (Grau is also from the Caribbean coast, being from Cartagena). Grau is also known for the minute detail of his work on the decorative elements in his paintings. Like Obregón, he did his most significant work in the 1960s, but his career spans from the 1940s to the 1990s. In the 1950s, Ramírez Villamizar did some of the most accomplished abstract geometrical painting to be completed in twentieth-century Colombia. Much of his painting can be understood as preparation for his later fine work as a sculptor.

Edgar Negret and Omar Rayo have also been major producers of abstract art in Colombia. Negret was an influential pioneer of abstract art in Colombia in the 1950s, and his work in painting and sculpture has been largely recognized in Colombia and abroad for its high quality. Rayo has been one of Colombia's most productive artists since the 1950s, with an ample work that has developed through several stages. He has successfully combined the abstract with the everyday, with strong influences of American pop and optic art since the 1960s.

The central and most accomplished figure of the generation to rise after World War II is Fernando Botero. Widely known for his robust figures, Botero is a master of satirical humor whose work is a synthesis of European classical traditions as well as folk traditions in Colombia. Consequently, Botero's work escapes simple classification as "modern" (or "traditional"), for it is a (modern) search for form that has been influenced by (traditional) painters such as Giotto, Piero, Michelangelo, and Velázquez. Botero has spoken of his dedication to form, in the tradition of the classic painters of Italy and Spain. His work has been recognized in Colombia since the 1950s and in Latin America, Europe, and the United States since the 1960s. He has also been quite prominent as a sculptor. In some ways, Botero has become for the plastic arts in Colombia what García Márquez has been for literature: an artist of exceptional imaginative power whose mastery of technique has allowed him to describe and invent a Colombian reality that he considers fantastic in a "realist" fashion—both Botero and García Márquez have spoken of their own work in this manner, considering themselves "realist" artists.

Since the 1940s, the situation of Colombian art has become more complex; painting has become more heterogeneous, and the number of artists has increased considerably. Figurative and experimental art both point in numerous directions, with a predominance of a variety of figurative boundaries in recent decades. Among these new directions, some are expressionist, others are metaphorical, few are surrealist, and others are considered classical, pop, realist, or political. The painters whose figurative work is expressionist are Leonel Góngora, Juan Antonio Roda, Manuel Estrada, Aníbal Gil, Angel Loochkartt, Teresa Cuéllar, Gerardo Aragón, Manuel Camargo, and Jorge Mantilla Caballero. Leonel Góngora has been active since the early 1960s in painting, drawing, and etching–works which signify his very personal style. His paintings are frequently erotic, and some Colombians have expressed the opinion that they are vulgar and pornographic.

The metaphoric expressionists in Colombia are Julio Castillo, Lucy Tejada, and Margarita Lozano. Castillo's work frequently exhibits an intention of being poetic, but he has been more successful in the marketing of commercial painting than the communication of deep meaning. His paintings tend to be of stylized human figures, often with emotional, tender overtones. Lucy Tejada has done work in painting, drawing, and etching, experimenting with a variety of forms and styles over the years. Margarita Lozano has been active since the 1960s; many of her paintings are of children and flowers, both of which she paints with bright colors and impressive skill.

The figurative painters who work in a surrealist mode are Rodolfo Velásquez and Alicia Viteri. Velásquez dedicated the early part of his career to drawing, but in recent years has been painting. In many of his paintings, he superimposes two images: In the lower part, he paints scenery to create a specific atmosphere, and in the upper part, he places an everyday object, such as a telephone, mirror, or newspaper. The juxtaposition of these two images becomes suggestive, and the clash between them can be quite surprising.

The "classical" or more traditional figurative painters are Juan Cárdenas, Luis Caballero, Gregorio Cuartas, and Antonio Barrera. The painting of Juan Cárdenas has been focused on the human body—usually his own. In some of his paintings he portrays a mimetic representation of the body; in others, outlines of bodies. Cárdenas has also worked on interior settings with antique objects, as well as some urban scenes. Luis Caballero has firm connections with classical painters, beginning with Michelangelo. Nevertheless, his figurative work is also closely allied with modern painting in general and contemporary expressionism in particular. He has been exhibiting his work in Europe and the United States since the mid–1960s, frequently with erotic scenes outlining human bodies. Living in Paris, Caballero has remained close to European painting from the Renaissance to the nineteenth century. Antonio Barrera has dedicated himself to painting landscapes since the 1970s, but he goes beyond the traditional realism of most landscapes, exploring abstract and surrealist approaches to his settings.

The figurative "pop" painters are Beatriz González, Alvaro Barrios, and Mónica Meira. After beginning a career in the mid–1960s using classical models, Beatriz González has cultivated a variety of pop forms, using an entire gamut of materials, from wood and tin to *esmalte* (enamel). She has successfully employed used furniture as the frame for much of her work, as well as cloths of different textures. Alvaro Barrios is a master of the art of drawing who has successfully projected juxtapositions of the everyday with the nostalgic and erotic. Meira began exhibiting her work in the 1970s, emphasizing everyday objects, and presenting them with an occasional humorous note.

The figurative painters working along more realist lines have been Alfredo Guerrero, Santiago Cárdenas, Darío Morales, Oscar Jaramillo, Mariana Varela, Cecilia Delgado, Miguel Angel Rojas, Martha Rodríguez, and Oscar Muñoz. After an initial stage experimenting with neorealism, Alfredo Guerrero has done fine work in realist portraits, many of himself or of nude women. Santiago Cárdenas began in the 1960s with pop realist paintings of bathers and women in automobiles. He has also done realist paintings of everyday objects with some experiments with trompe l'oeil. Darío Morales has dedicated a career to painting in Paris. Most of his early paintings of the 1970s were of nude women; since then, he has painted portraits and nude males. His work has been amply recognized in Latin America and Europe in the 1980s and 1990s. Since the mid–1970s, Cecilia Delgado has been painting the walls of older homes in Bogotá and Cartagena, emphasizing contrasts in light and shadow. Martha Rodríguez is known for her hyperrealist drawings, usually of human faces.

The two most outstanding figurative painters who work on political themes are Luis Angel Rengifo and Pedro Alcántara. Rengifo has produced a broad range of paintings, but he is particularly well known for his drawings dealing with La Violencia. Alcántara has worked with obvious political intentions, attempting to increase the political awareness of those who see his work. He has been exhibiting drawings since the 1960s, and they are characterized by his technical skill and absolute control of the curved line.

Colombian writers, such as R. H. Moreno-Durán and Albalucía Angel, have experimented with the postmodern, and the same can be said of Colombian creators working in the plastic arts. Nevertheless, Colombian artists (like its writers) have not been particularly interested in avant-garde experimentation to the extent that such has taken place since the 1960s in the United States and Europe. Feliza Bursztyn has made sculpture with metal trash, and Tiberio Vanegas has worked with glass fiber. María Teresa Negreiros has produced some tridimensional experiments with occasional allusions to op art. Julia Acuña has mounted light and sound spectacles with movement. At the same time, young Colombian artists have occasionally experimented with pop art, happenings, conceptual art, and even ecological art. Generally speaking, Colombia's most successful and recognized painters have assimilated American and European modernity quite well, but have been followers rather than innovators since Obregón, Botero, and Grau.

Colombian sculpture has not been as prominent as painting. Nevertheless, there has been a small group of sculptors active in Colombia since the 1930s. The most recognized of these twentieth-century sculptors have been Pedro Nel Gómez, Rodrigo Arenas Betancur, Edgar Negret, Eduardo Ramírez Villamizar, Luis Alberto Acuña, Obregón, Botero, Morales, Amaral, and Villegas. After studying in Europe in the 1920s, Pedro Nel Gómez returned to Colombia in 1930; he became best known for his mural paintings on public buildings in Medellín. The major portion of his most important muralistic work appeared in the 1940s and 1950s. Later in his career, however, he also worked occasionally on sculpture projects. For example, from 1970 to 1973, he worked on a sculpture for the National University in Medellín titled *Totem mítico* (*Mythical Totem*). Recognized primarily as a muralist and painter, Gómez nevertheless completed enough sculpture with some universal and mythological references to the Americas that in 1978 a book was published dedicated to the study of his sculpture.

Rodrigo Arenas Betancur is the most recognized sculptor in Colombia for his monumental public works. Trained in Mexico, he brought the tradition of the grandiose public monuments that flourished after the Mexican Revolution. His monuments are typically constructed of bronze or cement, and frequently carry patriotic and social messages. His human figures are often launched upward into the air with a sense of purpose, and sometimes even aggression.

Two painters who have been major figures in sculpture are Edgar Negret and Eduardo Ramírez Villamizar. Negret has assembled metal constructions with a simultaneously mechanical and animal-like appearance. Negret's aluminum structures tend to be geometric in form, but they sometimes also evoke the Baroque tradition in Latin America, as well as living forms.

Ramírez Villamizar began as a painter in the 1950s, but his artistic career became increasingly oriented toward sculpture. He is more systematically ordered and rational in his approach than Negret, remaining closer to classical forms. He also assimilates more from the Colombian tradition than Negret. Ramírez Villamizar is also more of a purist of form, frequently using geometric forms on his work with wood, metal, or cement. Since beginning to work on sculpture in the 1960s, he has become one of Colombia's major sculptors, where he is particularly known for his large works of monumental dimensions. His work has been exhibited throughout Colombia and the Americas, including some of the most prestigious galleries and museums in the United States.

Several other sculptors have had some presence in Colombia over the past twenty years. Carlos Rojas shares some of the purist interests in geometric forms of Ramírez Villamizar, creating sculptures of the minimalist school.

John Castles has explored conceptual spaces with his steel pieces. Ronny Vayda has been working on projects with steel and glass, and Germán Botero with cubical structures. Other sculptors are Héctor F. Oviedo, Gabriel Beltrán, and Celso Román.

When President Belisario Betancur organized the exhibition of young Colombian painters working abroad, this show revealed the vitality of Colombian painting on the international scenario. Among the painters selected as the most accomplished were Eduardo Hosie (1953), Luis Eduardo Garzón (1954), Juliana Cuéllar (1956), Yolanda Mesa (1953), and Juana Pérez (1951).

PHOTOGRAPHY

The history of Colombian photography began in the 1860s, when several small commercial operations opened their doors to the photographing of portraits. Entrepreneurs such as Gonzalo Gaviria in Bogotá, Tomás Acevedo in Medellín, and J. G. Gutiérrez Ponce in Cali provided families with the opportunity to comply with the latest fashion learned from European photographers who had been in Colombia in 1855–1856: the family portrait. Colombians had been hearing about this new European technology since the news of photography first appeared in the Colombian press in 1839.

During the early years of photography in Colombia, virtually all photographic activity involved portraits. In fact, approximately 95 percent of the pictures taken in Colombia from the 1860s to the 1880s were portraits. The magazine *Papel Periódico Ilustrado* provided the first opportunity for Colombian photographers to explore beyond the genre of the family portrait. The main photographer hired by this magazine was Julio Racines, who took pictures mostly of the landscape. This magazine also published photographs taken by Demetrio Paredes and a few others. Besides picturesque views of the Colombian countryside, the *Papel Periódico Ilustrado* also featured pictures of an earthquake in Cúcuta, a fire in Bogotá, and religious processions on Sundays.

After this initial stage of Colombia's photographic infancy, Melitón Rodríguez, the giant of Colombian photography, appeared on the scene. Once his work surfaced in 1891, he dominated Colombian photography until 1938 and, in the process, made himself the central figure of this century.

Melitón Rodríguez was a commercial photographer who used his genius to make photography an art form. He followed the commercial path of making family portraits, but his work went far beyond the tradition of family portraits that he inherited, creating a photographic history of the city of Medellín and Antioquia. As a visual historian, Rodríguez left a record of the transformation of Medellín and the society of Antioquia from 1892 to 1938. He took superb pictures of everything from the most important buildings to everyday scenes, such as the kitchen of a private home.

Rodríguez's pictures of people also covered a broad range. On one hand, he took photographs of common people and workers in a variety of settings. On the other hand, he left a superb visual record of Antioquia's most celebrated writers and political figures. He photographed writers such as the poet León de Greiff and the novelist Juan José Botero. His pictures of political figures included Rafael Uribe Uribe, a famous leader of the War of a Thousand Days (1899–1902) and the model García Márquez used for the creation of the character the colonel Aureliano Buendía. Another of Rodríguez's masterful photos is of union leader and writer María Cano. Viewed in retrospect, Rodríguez's photographic work is not only the most important of the twentieth century in Colombia, but quite significant in Latin America in general.

Late nineteenth- and early twentieth-century photography in Colombia included one more facet besides individual portraits and the work of Melitón Rodríguez. Colombian photographers recorded the civil war experience with their art. Since Melitón Rodríguez and the civil wars, however, Colombian photography has not been in any way as exceptional as it was the first half of the century; there are no world-class photographers in Colombia today.

ARCHITECTURE

Colombia has never produced anything particularly new or innovative to the international architectural community, according to one of Colombia's authoritative critics of architecture.[1] Unlike some of its most creative writers and painters, such as García Márquez and Obregón, Colombian architects have been known primarily as professionals who have adopted and assimilated the work of European, North American, and Latin American architects. Nevertheless, Colombian architecture has produced heterogeneous and often noteworthy urban spaces, buildings, and residences in Colombia, making considerable progress and moving into the realm of postmodern constructs in recent years.

Unlike literature and plastic arts (where there is little common agreement among critics about the exact nature of the developments of movements, such as modernism), in Colombian architecture the lines of development can be more clearly classified into three periods: colonial, *republicano*, and modern. Colonial architecture covers the three centuries of Spanish rule in the region of New Granada; *republicano* architecture spans from the nineteenth century until approximately the 1920s; modern architecture began in the 1930s and has continued in a variety of modes (including a postmodern variant) throughout

the remainder of the century. In general, less than ideal continuity has characterized each of these three modes; the potential marriage between form and
function has also been, generally speaking, less than ideal in Colombia.

The remains of colonial architecture are still to be found in many urban
spaces of Colombia, mostly in the form of churches built by the Spaniards in
the sixteenth, seventeenth, and eighteenth centuries. These churches were imi-
tations of their Medieval and Renaissance models in Spain, and tended to be
gothic and neoclassic structures with occasional influences of local indigenous
cultures. The "La Candelaria" neighborhood in Bogotá, as well as large sections of Cartagena, Tunja, and Popayán have preserved entire sections of colonial urban design, with narrow streets and residences typically no more than
one or two stories. Indeed, one of Colombia's most progressive tourist attrac-
tions (for Colombians and foreigners alike) is the "old city" section of Cartagena, which is a Spanish colonial urban space entirely preserved and inhabited
by urban dwellers. The town of Santa Fe de Antioquia, located in rural Antioquia, is also predominantly colonial in architecture. (Popayán's original colonial structures were destroyed by an earthquake in the early 1980s; since then,
the city has been reconstructed in the traditional colonial mode.)

In the nineteenth century, Colombian urban spaces were not conceived by
architects in the modern sense, but planned and pieced together by artisans.
Today, both urban and rural spaces have some remnants of nineteenth-century
republicano architecture, which had declared itself, from the beginning, independent of the models and lines of the colonial architecture associated with
Spanish rule. The national capitol building in Bogotá, the Palacio de Nariño,
as well as a large number of government buildings still used throughout the nation, were built in the *republicano* style. This nineteenth-century architecture
was eclectic in style, drawing from Greek, Roman, and Renaissance lines that
were also to be found in the architecture of the same period in the United States
and Europe. *Republicano* architecture also replaced the old style with new materials: cement became an important element in Colombian buildings for the
first time, as well as steel.

The rise of modern architecture in Colombia began in the 1930s with the
modernization of Colombian society in general by a series of presidents of the
Liberal Party, beginning with Presidents Enrique Olaya Herrera (1930–1934)
and Alfonso López Pumarejo (1934–1938). Progressive liberals Olaya Herrera, López Pumarejo, and their cohorts visualized the new ideas in urban design as an opportunity to reject the conservative past by demolishing many
extant colonial structures. Consequently, the demolition of the Convento
Santo Domingo in Bogotá was both a symbolic act and a politically motivated
transformation of the urban scenery in Bogotá. The symbolism involved with

Republican-style architecture in rural Antioquia

destroying colonial architecture in Colombia was multilayered, for it was a self-conscious attempt to eradicate a past that the liberal majority considered conservative, Catholic, colonial, and Hispanic.

The foundation of the School of Architecture in the Universidad Nacional in 1936 also was an important factor in the ongoing modernization of urban spaces in Colombia. Headed by Carlos Martínez, the School of Architecture trained the first generation of professional architects; they tended to be international in vision and tastes, promoting ideas in Colombia about the new modern architecture in vogue in Europe and the United States.

In the 1930s, new concepts of urban space, urban development, and public housing began appearing in Colombia. The centenary of 1938 created an atmosphere supporting innovation and change. The presence of the Austrian Karl Brunner in Bogotá in the 1920s had a significant impact on nascent ideas about urban space. In the 1930s, two urban spaces were set aside for planned development with a specific urban design in mind: the Parque Nacional and the Universidad Nacional. In the latter, several buildings were representative of the modernization of architecture in Colombia. In Medellín, Pedro Nel Gómez designed the Palacio Municipal, an eclectic building with both old and new lines of architecture. Gómez's work emphasized indigenous and nationalistic values.

Residence from the 1920s in Barranquilla

The very idea of public housing was new to Colombia in this period, and was the beginning of a new awareness of the need for public housing in urban areas, which has reached crisis proportions since the massive immigration of the rural population into urban areas since the late 1940s. (This general trend toward urban immigration in Latin America was exacerbated in Colombia with the undeclared civil war of La Violencia from 1948 to 1958, which resulted in much of the rural population moving to the cities to avoid widespread rural violence.) One of the pioneer efforts in high-density public housing was the Centro Urbano Antonio Nariño, which was conceived in the late 1940s and constructed from 1950 to 1953.

By the 1940s, many of the new ideas about modern architecture were put into practice. The ideas of Le Corbusier had an enormous impact in Colombia, and his arrival in Bogotá in 1947 resulted in an emphasis on his ideas about the use of light and simplicity. Similarly, the presence of Frank Lloyd Wright was increasingly visible. Neighborhoods with residences reflecting these new conceptions of architecture were constructed in Bogotá ("Teusaquillo"), Barranquilla ("El Prado"), Cali ("Centenario"), and Cartagena ("Bocagrande"). Following the slogans of Le Corbusier (which young Colombian architects often repeated), the homes in these residential neighborhoods integrated a play

Medellín

with sunlight, with intentions of making the home a "machine for living." Carlos Martínez and Jorge Arango promoted such ideas in the architecture magazine *Proa*, which they founded.

In the 1950s and 1960s, the modernization of Colombia's urban spaces continued along these same lines, with an increased influence of American architectural ideas and "corporate aesthetics." The American firm Skidmore, Owings, and Merrill, which offered consulting work in Colombia, soon had Colombian equivalents, such as Herrera y Nieto Cano. Most of these firms, such as Obregón y Valenzuela, did not give thorough consideration to the particular Colombian contexts in which they were operating. Consequently, the new corporate aesthetics were often more a reflection of the firm's conceptualization of an ideal urban space than an adequate response to the architectural setting and its needs.

Despite these disparities, there were some interesting successes in Colombian architecture in the 1960s, some of the most noteworthy being the auditorium of the Biblioteca Luis Angel Arango, which is both visually attractive and ideal in acoustics for concerts. In this sense, the Biblioteca Luis Angel Arango is a superb example of the ideal marriage of form and function to be found in Colombia.

The skyscraper also arrived in Colombia in the 1960s, beginning with the forty-floor Avianca building in downtown Bogotá, where the tallest building before its completion in 1966 had twenty-three floors. This technical innovation (for Colombia) in the use of glass and steel soon had reproductions in Medellín and Cali. In Medellín, the first such skyscraper was the Coltejer building.

The urban spaces of Colombia suffered from symptoms of crisis and chaos in the 1970s and 1980s. A lack of consistent and coherent urban planning increased traffic problems, as well as pollution and noise. With the different cycles of an always fragile economy, unemployment and severe underemployment often resulted in street crime and petty street violence in Bogotá, Medellín, and Cali. With the crackdown on the drug cartels in the late 1980s and 1990s, urban violence was severe in Bogotá and Medellín. Bombings in the streets of Bogotá during the drug wars of the late 1980s created a war mentality among urban dwellers. One of the most commented upon grafitti was a reference to Bogotá as "Apenas Sudamericana" (barely South American), a parody of the capital city as the *Atenas Sudamericana* (Athens of South America).

From the mid–1980s to the mid–1990s, there was a "boom" in the construction of luxurious new private residences and commercial buildings, many of which were financed, directly or indirectly, with the influx of dollars from the illegal drug trade. Nevertheless, this construction boom of the 1980s and 1990s transformed much of the urban space of Colombia, providing it with a postmodern glitter and glaze (as well as a few new buildings with postmodern lines). In many ways, Colombia's urban space was improved with the postmodernization of Bogotá, Medellín, Cali, and Barranquilla. Sleek and fashionable condominium buildings even appeared in smaller cities, such as Manizales and Pereira.

At the turn of the twenty-first century, Colombian architecture and urban designing is as varied and heterogeneous as anywhere. Colonial, modern, and postmodern lines can be seen in juxtaposition in many of Colombia's urban settings. More than in any period of Colombia's history, both private and public entities are fully committed to protecting and preserving the colonial, the modern, and the postmodern that are all integral parts of Colombia's urban life.

Notes

CHAPTER 1: CONTEXT

1. In the review of Colombian literature in chapter 6, however, the interior highland is divided into two regions: the interior highland and greater Tolima. In general, it is most appropriate to consider the culture and society of the greater Tolima area as an extension of the interior highland. In chapter 6, the interior highland is divided into two regions to provide more detail of the literature of that specific area.

2. For further discussion of the uneven development of the Caribbean coastal area, see Orlando Fals Borda, *Historia doble de la costa*, vol. 1.

3. Friedemann and Patiño Roselli, *Lengua y sociedad en el Palenque de San Basilio*; Bickerton and Escalante, *Palenquero*; Megenney, *El palenquero*.

4. See Bickerton and Escalante, *Palenquero*; Megenney, *El palenquero*.

5. See Friedemann and Patiño Roselli, *Lengua y sociedad en el Palenque de San Basilio*; Megenney, *El palenquero*.

6. McGreevey, *An Economic History of Colombia*, p. 278.

7. Ibid., p. 245.

8. Núñez, *La federación*, pp. 7–8, 13.

9. Park, *Rafael Núñez and the Politics of Colombian Regionalism*, p. 7. In addition, Joseph L. Love, in a study of Latin American regionalism, emphasizes its importance in Colombia: "The problems of regional conflict—relationships of domination and subordination, the competition for scarce resources, and the tension between national integration and regional separatism—are of major importance in the history of Mexico, Brazil, and Colombia." Love, "An Approach to Regionalism," p. 138.

CHAPTER 2: RELIGION

1. See Blutstein et al., *Colombia: A Country Study* for further discussion of the pervasive influence of the Catholic Church in Colombian institutions and daily life. See in particular their affirmation (p. 138) that many scholars consider the influence of the church in the daily lives of Colombians and their institutions to be the most pervasive in the Western Hemisphere.

CHAPTER 3: SOCIAL CUSTOMS AND DAILY LIFE

1. For a more detailed review of clothing traditions in Colombia, see Jaramillo de Olarte and Trujillo Jaramillo, *Trece danzas tradicionales de Colombia: sus trajes y su música*.

2. For much of the information offered in this section on traditional Colombian dance, I am indebted to Jaramillo de Olarte and Trujillo Jaramillo, ibid.

3. See Montaña, *Fauna social colombiana*.

4. Pablo Escobar became such a legendary figure in Colombia that several entire books were published on him. See, for example, Fogel, *El testamento de Pablo Escobar*; Cañón M., *El patrón: vida y muerte de Pablo Escobar*; García, *Los barones de la cocaína*; Castillo, *Los jinetes de la cocaína*; and Pedro Casals, *Disparando cocaína*.

CHAPTER 4: THE MEDIA

1. Much of the statistical data and factual information about Colombian television come from the book published by *Inravisión*. See Stamato, *Historia de una travesía*.

2. Merrill, *Global Journalism*, p. 288.

3. Ibid., p. 292.

4. Stamato, *Historia de una travesía*, p. 436.

5. Ibid., p. 444.

6. Ibid., p. 453.

7. The schematic divisions of the history of Colombian radio of both Reynaldo Pareja and Hernando Téllez B., as presented in their respective books, have been combined and condensed here. See bibliography.

8. de la Espriella Ossío, *Historia de la música en Colombia a través de nuestro bolero*, p. 453.

9. Téllez B., *Cincuenta años de radiodifusión colombiana*, 1974.

10. Parejo, *Historia de la radio en Colombia: 1929–1980*, p. 125.

11. Cacua Prada, *Historia del periodismo colombiano*, p. 20.

12. Otero Muñoz, *Historia del periodismo en Colombia*, p. 37.

13. Cacua Prada, "*La Bagatela*," p. 68.

14. More information and details of many of the Colombian newspapers of the nineteenth century mentioned in this chapter can be found in the book by Gustavo Otero Muñoz. See bibliography.

15. Fonnegra, *La prensa en Colombia*, p. 21.

16. Ibid., p. 29.

CHAPTER 6: LITERATURE

1. The associations between the interior highland and greater Tolima are so close, in fact, that the greater Tolima is included here as an extension of the interior highland in the original description of the regions of Colombia (see chapter 1). In this chapter, greater Tolima is more specifically referred to as a cultural entity in order to deal in more detail with the literature of this region.

2. For a more detailed discussion of the function of the narrator and the role of the author figure in *La vorágine*, see Raymond L. Williams, *The Colombian Novel, 1844–1987*. In this book, the Colombian novel, within its regional context, is covered in far more detail than is possible here.

CHAPTER 7: GABRIEL GARCÍA MÁRQUEZ: THE WRITER AND THE MAN

1. García Márquez returned to Colombia in 1982 after making a special arrangement with President Belisario Betancur to provide him with security assistance. Since he intended to stay in Cartagena much of the time in the 1980s when he was in Colombia, security was not a difficult problem, for Cartagena has generally been free of violence and kidnappings. Nevertheless, in the late 1980s and early 1990s, García Márquez found security a serious problem, for even the presidents of Colombia have not been able to guarantee his safety in a nation with one of the highest kidnapping and homicide rates in the West.

2. I have known García Márquez personally since the early 1980s. In the 1990s, I have noticed a change in his attitude toward his professional readers and critics. In the fall of 1996, he accepted an invitation to meet in Guadalajara, Mexico, for a week to engage scholars of his work in a dialogue. I participated in that discussion and noted that he was quite generous when speaking of literary critics.

3. Magic realist fiction in Latin America has origins in the 1940s. For a complete overview of magic realism, see Menton, *Magic Realism Rediscovered, 1918–1982*; and Parkinson Zamora and Faris, eds., *Magical Realism: Theory, History, Community*.

4. For a more precise chronological overview of the development of García Márquez's literature of Macondo, see Williams, *Gabriel García Márquez.*.

5. Williams, *Gabriel García Márquez*, p. 21.

6. Ibid., p. 22.

7. García Márquez made this statement in an interview with E. González Bermejo, "Ahora 200 años de soledad," *Oiga*, no. 392 (September 1970): 31.

8. For a more detailed discussion of the move from preliteracy to literacy in *One Hundred Years of Solitude*, see Raymond L. Williams, *The Colombian Novel, 1844–1987*, chapter 4.

CHAPTER 8: THE PLASTIC ARTS, PHOTOGRAPHY, AND ARCHITECTURE

1. See Germán Téllez, "La arquitectura y el urbanismo en la época actual," p. 386.

Glossary

agua aromática: Type of herbal tea.

aguardiente: Corn or sugar brandy.

ajiaco: Stew with three types of potato, chicken, and corn.

antioqueño: From Antioquia.

arroz con coco: Rice dish cooked in coconut oil.

autocensura: Self-consorship.

Balada: Ballad.

bamboleo: Traditional music form of the western coast.

bambuco: Traditional music and dance of the interior highland.

bandeja paisa: Typical dish of Antioquia consisting of beans, rice, potatoes, ground beef, pork rinds, and eggs.

bogotanos: People from Bogotá.

bolero: Traditional Spanish music and dance form with numerous variations in Latin American countries.

bullerengue: Traditional music and dance form of the Caribbean coast.

café: Coffee with warm milk.

café/librería: Coffee house/bookstore.

caleños: People from Cali.

campesino: Peasant, farmer.

caudillo: Local chief, military leader, or head of state.

cepillao: Dance step in the *guabina*.

chupas: Shirt.

cine independiente: Independent film.

cine marginal: Marginal film.

cine militante: Militant film.

Colombia linda: Beautiful Colombia.

contradanza: Traditional music form of the western coast.

cordilleras: Mountain ranges.

costeño: From the coastal region.

costumbrista: Regional literature celebrating local customs.

criollista: Literature of the 1920s and 1930s that emphasized issues of national identity and regional values.

criollos: Caucasians of Spanish bloodlines born in Colombia.

crónico social: Short documentary work in the film industry.

cuchuco: Dish prepared from wheat grits and pork.

cumbia: Traditional music and dance of the Caribbean coast.

cuña: Commercial time slot in radio or television.

cununo: Drum used in dances in greater Cauca.

currulao: Traditional dance and music form of the western coast.

escribiente: Scribe.

escuela antioqueña: School of literature from the department of Antioquia.

esmalte: Enamel, glaze.

fiestas: Holiday celebrations or parties.

fondongo: Representative musical form of Colombia.

fula: Mantilla of velvet-like cloth.

fútbol: Soccer.

gaita: Bagpipe (literally); Musical form that includes the bagpipe.

galerón: Traditional music form of the llanos (plains).

gallinazo: Vulture (literally); Don Juan-type who chases women.

garabato: Representative musical form of Colombia.

gran prensa, la: The great press.

gringo: (pejorative) Foreigner.

guabina: Traditional music and dance of the interior highland.

guayabera: Loose-fitting flowery shirt.

joropo: Traditional music form of the llanos (plains).

lagarto: Lizard (literally); social climber who abuses social situations.

llamador: "Caller" drum in the *mapalé* dance.

llanos: Plains.

lobo: Wolf (literally); lower-class social climber, lacking in refinement.

manjar blanco: Traditional dessert made of sweet milk curds.

manta: Piece of cloak.

mapalé: Traditional dance and music form of the Caribbean coast.

mar: Sea.

merengue: Musical form of the Dominican Republic.

mestizo: Mixture of Spanish and Indian influences.

mondongo: Dish of tripe.

Mundial de Fútbol: World Cup in soccer.

nadaísmo: Avant-garde and experimental literary movement of the late 1950s and 1960s.

nadaísta: Writer of the *nadaísmo* movement.

narco-curas: Priests paid by drug traffickers.

narco-guerrillas: Leftist guerrillas related to drug traffickers.

narco-poetas: Poets who write verse in praise of drug traffickers.

novilladas: Bullfights performed by beginning professionals.

nuevo cine colombiano: New Colombian film.

palanca: "In" or "inside track"; personal connection of leverage.

palenquero: Spanish-based creole language spoken in the *palenques.*

palenques: Villages founded by black rebels.

panela: Brown sugar.

paseo: Representative music and dance form of Colombia.

pasillo: Traditional music form of the interior highland region.

perico: Small cup of coffee with a dash of milk.

plaga maravillosa: Marvelous plague.

plaza de toros: Bullring.

porro: Representative musical form of Colombia.

presentadora: Entertainment show hostess.

presidentes gramáticos: Presidents who were men of letters with training in classical literatures.

puente: Bridge (literally); a three-day weekend.

puya: Representative musical form of Colombia.

radionovela: Radio soap opera.

radioperiódico: Radio newscast.

rancheras: Traditional musical form of Mexico.

Reinado de Belleza: Beauty contest.

ruana: Cloak worn draped over the shoulders.

salsa: Music and dance form of the Caribbean.

sancocho: Fish or chicken stew made in the Caribbean region.

sobrebarriga: Type of flank steak marinated in a special sauce.

Suaza (hat): Typical hat of the interior highland region.

tambor mayor: Main drum.

telenovela: Prime-time soap opera.

tercer cine: Third World film.

tierra caliente: Hot lowlands.

tinto: Black coffee.

torbellino: Traditional dance of the interior highland.

vallenato: Popular musical form of Colombia.

Bibliography

Bickerton, Derek, and Aquiles Escalante. *Palenquero: A Spanish-Based Creole of North Colombia. Lingua 24*. Amsterdam: North Holland Publishing Company, 1970.

Blutstein, Howard I., J. David Edwards, Kathryn Therese Johnston, David S. McMorris, and James D. Rudolph. *Colombia: A Country Study*. Washington, D.C.: U.S. Government Printing Office, 1976.

Cacua Prada, Antonio. *Historia del periodismo colombiano*. Bogotá: N.P., 1968.

———. *Doscientos años: orígenes del periodismo colombiano*. Bogotá: Editorial Kelly, 1991.

———. *Correo Curioso* (prologue). Bogotá: Facsimilar de la Biblioteca Nacional, 1993.

———. *La Bagatela*: Primer periódico político en la Nueva Granada. *Investigación y Desarrollo Social*. Bogotá: Universidad Militar Nueva Granada, 1994, pp. 63–88.

Cañón M., Luis. *El patrón: vida y muerte de Pablo Escobar*. Bogotá: Planeta, 1994.

Casals, Pedro. *Disparando cocaína*. Bogotá: Plaza y Janés, 1986.

Castaño Castillo, Alvaro, director. *Cronología de la cultura 1950–1990*. Bogotá: Villega Editores, 1990.

Castillo, Fabio. *Los jinetes de la cocaína*. Bogotá: Editorial Documentos Periodísticos, 1987.

de la Espriella Ossío, Alfonso. *Historia de la música en Colombia a través de nuestro bolero*. Bogotá: Editorial Norma, 1997.

de la Torre, Cristina. *Juicio a la televisión colombiana*. Bogotá: Editorial Nikos and Editorial Oveja Negra, 1985.

Fals Borda, Orlando. *Historia doble de la costa*. 4 vols. Bogotá: Carlos Valencia Editores, 1979.

Fogel, Jean-François. *El testamento de Pablo Escobar.* Bogotá: Intermedio Editores, 1994.

Fonnegra, Gabriel. *La prensa en Colombia.* Bogotá: El Ancora Editores, 1984.

Friedemann, Nina S., and Carlos Patiño Roselli. *Lengua y sociedad en el Palenque de San Basilio.* Bogotá: Publicaciones del Instituto Caro y Cuervo, 1983.

García, Miguel. *Los barones de la cocaína.* Bogotá: Planeta, 1991.

González Bermejo, E. "Ahora 200 años de soledad." *Oiga*, 392 (September 1970): 31.

Gutiérrez Azopardo, Ildefonso. *Historia del negro en Colombia.* Bogotá: Editorial Nueva América, 1986.

Jaramillo de Olarte, Lucía, and Mónica Trujillo Jaramillo. *Trece danzas tradicionales de Colombia: sus trajes y su música.* Bogotá: Fondo Cultural Cafetero, 1991.

Love, Joseph L. "An Approach to Regionalism." In *New Approaches to Latin American History.* Edited by Richard Graham and Peter Smith. Austin: University of Texas Press, 1974, pp. 137–155.

McGreevey, William Paul. *An Economic History of Colombia.* Cambridge: Cambridge University Press, 1971.

Megenney, William W. *El palenquero: un lenguaje post-criollo de Colombia.* Bogotá: Instituto Caro y Cuervo, 1986.

Menton, Seymour. *Magic Realism Rediscovered, 1918–1982.* Philadelphia: Art Alliance Press, 1983.

Merrill, John C., ed. *Global Journalism.* New York: Longman, 1991.

Montaña, Antonio. *Fauna social colombiana.* Bogotá: Ediciones Gamma, 1988.

Mutis Durán, Santiago, ed. *Manual de historia de Colombia.* 3 vols. Bogotá: Procultura/Instituto Colombiano de Cultura, 1982.

Núñez, Rafael. *La federación.* Bogotá: N.P., 1885.

Otero Muñoz. Gustavo. *Historia del periodismo en Colombia.* Bogotá: Universidad Sergio Arboleda, 1998.

Pareja, Reynaldo. *Historia de la radio en Colombia: 1929–1980.* Bogotá: Servicio Colombiano de Comunicación Social, 1984.

Park, James W. *Rafael Núñez and the Politics of Colombian Regionalism.* Baton Rouge: Louisiana State University Press, 1985.

Parkinson Zamora, Lois, and Wendy B. Faris, eds. *Magical Realism: Theory, History, Community.* Durham: Duke University Press, 1995.

Perl, Matthias, and Armin Schwegler, eds. *América negra: panorámica actual de los estudios lingüísticos sobre variedades hispanas, portuguesas y criollas.* Frankfurt: Vervuert Verlag, 1998.

Sorela, Pedro. *El otro García Márquez. Los años difíciles.* Madrid: Mondadori, 1988.

Stamato, Vicente, ed. *Historia de una travesía: cuarenta años de la televisión en Colombia.* Bogotá: Instituto Nacional de Radio y Televisión, 1994.

Téllez, Germán. "La arquitectura y el urbanismo en la época actual," in Santiago Mutis Durán, ed., *Manual de historia de Colombia.* Bogotá: Procultura/Instituto Colombiano de Cultura, 1982, pp. 343–444.

Téllez B., Hernando. *Cincuenta años de radiodifusión colombiana.* Bogotá: N.P., 1974.

Ulloa, Alejandro. *La salsa en Cali.* Cali: Universidad del Valle, 1992.

Williams, Raymond L. *Gabriel García Márquez.* Boston: G. K. Hall, 1984.

———. *The Colombian Novel: 1844–1987.* Austin: University of Texas Press, 1991.

———. *The Postmodern Novel in Latin America.* New York: St. Martin's Press, 1995.

Index

Acosta de Samper, Soledad, 37, 60, 80, 85
Acuña, Julia, 122
Acuña, Luis Alberto, 118, 123
Agricultural products, 12–13
Aguilera Garramuño, Marco Tulio, 95
AID (Agencia Internacional para el Desarrollo), 48
Albarracín, Jacinto, 70
Alcántara, Pedro, 122
Alvarez, Carlos, 67
Alvarez, Lily, 65
Alvarez Gardeazábal, Gustavo, 67, 80, 91–94
Alvarez Lleras, Antonio, 70
Amaral, Olga de, 118, 123
Amore, Italo, 50
Amórtegui, Jesús, 50
ANDA (Asociación Nacional de Anunciantes), 47
Angel, Albalucía, 38, 94–95
ANRADIO (Asociación Nacional de Radiodifusión), 54
Aragón, Gerardo, 120
Arango, Gonzalo, 71, 93
Arango, Jorge Luis, 44
Arango de Tobón, Graciela, 75

Arboleda, Julio, 59
Arboleda, Sergio, 11
Architecture, 125–130; colonial, 126; modernization, 127–130; public housing, 128; *republicano*, 126–127
Arenas Betancur, Rodrigo, 123
Artel, Jorge, 83
Arzuaga, José María, 66
Azuola y Lozano, José Luis de, 58

Barba Jacob, Porfirio (Miguel Angel Osorio), 85
Barco, Virgilio, 12
Barrera, Antonio, 121
Barrios, Alvaro, 121
Barros, José, 75
Beltrán, Gabriel, 124
Bermúdez, Lucho, 75
Betancur, Belisario, 38, 79, 92, 97, 103, 117
Bogotazo, 53–54, 56, 61
Bolívar, Simón, 10, 59
Botero, Fernando, xvi, 117, 120, 123
Botero, Germán, 124
Brunner, Karl, 127
Buenaventura, Enrique, 63, 71–72
Buitrago, Fanny, 38, 93

Bursztyn, Feliza, 122

Caballero, Luis, 121
Caballero Calderón, Eduardo, 54, 88
Cabrera, Sergio, 68
Caicedo, Andrés, 68, 95
Caldas, Francisco José de, 58
Caldas, Susana, 37
Calvo, Máximo, 65
Camacho, Joaquín, 58
Camacho Ramírez, Arturo, 86
Camargo, Manuel, 120
Cano, Fidel, 60
Cano, Guillermo, 61
Cano, María, 124
CARACOL (Cadena Radial Colombiana), 55–56
Cárdenas, Juan, 121
Cárdenas, Santiago, 122
Caribbean coastal region: history and features, 4; traditional clothing, 29; traditional dance, 32–33; traditional music, 73. *See also* Literature
Caro, José Eusebio, 11
Caro, Miguel Antonio, 10, 79, 86, 92
Caro, Rufino José, 11
Carranza, Eduardo, 86
Carranza, María Mercedes, 38
Carrasquilla, Tomás, 9, 25-26, 65, 71, 84–85
Cartels, 13, 36, 40–41
Carvajal, Mario, 90
Castañeda Aragón, Gregorio, 83
Castaño Castillo, Alvaro, 54
Castellanos, Dora, 86
Castillo, Julio, 121
Castles, John, 124
Castro Saavedra, Carlos, 86
Cepeda, Angie, 37
Cepeda Samudio, Alvaro, 37, 82, 84, 93; film and, 65–66; theater and, 72
"El Chinche Ulloa," 75
CICA (Círculo Colombiano de Actores), 45

Cinema, 63–68; contemporary film, 67–68; *criollista* films, 65; film boom, 66; first sound films, 65; professionalization and growth, 67; silent films, 64–65
Collazos, Oscar, 94
Colombia linda, 25
Cote Lemus, Eduardo, 86–87
Cuartas, Gregorio, 121
Cuéllar, Juliana, 124
Cuéllar, Teresa, 120
Cuervo, Angel, 87
Cuervo, Rufino José, 86
Customs, urban social, 38–40

Dance, traditional and regional, 31–33
De la Espriella, Alfredo, 71
De la Peña, Brother Francisco, 57
De la Rosa, Amira, 71
Delgado, Cecilia, 122
Delmar, Meira, 83
Del Socorro Rodríguez, Manuel, 57
Díaz, Diomedes, 74
Díaz, Eugenio, 85–86
Di Domenicos, 64
Distefano, Alfredo, 35
Dress and traditional costumes, 27–28
Drug trafficking, xv-xvi; cartels, 13, 36, 40–41; culture, 40–41; Escobar, Pablo, 13, 40–41, 48; media and, 48, 61
Dugand, Nacho, 75
Duque, Lisandro, 68
Duque López, Alberto, 68, 95
Durán, Alejo, 74
Durán, Ciro, 66

Echavarría, Rogelio, 85
Echeverri, Raúl ("Jorgito"), 52
Eco, 93
Economy, 12–13
Escalona, Rafael, 73–74
Escobar, Pablo, 13, 40–41, 48
Escobar Giraldo, Octavio, 96
Espinosa, Germán, 94

Estefan, Gloria, 63, 76
Estrada, Manuel, 120

Fajardo, Julio José, 86
Fernández de Valenzuela, Fernando, 69
Fernández Madrid, José, 69–70
Festivities, national and regional, 29–31
Fiestas, 26
Film. *See* Cinema
Food consumption and regional cuisine, 33–35
Fuenmayor, Alfonso, 66, 82, 99
Fuenmayor, José Félix, 9, 82–84

Gaitán, Jorge Eliécer, 12, 17, 53
Gaitán Durán, Jorge, 86–87
Gamboa, Octavio, 86, 90
García, Jaime, 51
García, Santiago, 66, 71
García Herreros, Manuel, 83–84
García Márquez, Gabriel: early life, 97–99; film, 65-66, 68, 100–102; "Group of Barranquilla," 37, 66, 82, 99, 102, 118; journalism, 56–57, 98–100; Nobel Prize, xvi, 97; profession of writing, 98–99; *vallenato*, 74; writers of the Boom and, 101–102. Fiction: early writings, 103–106; literature of Macondo, 106–114; post-Macondo works, 114–116. Works: *The Autumn of the Patriarch*, 114–116; *Big Mama's Funeral*, 98, 109–111; *Chronicle of a Death Foretold*, 114–116; *The General in His Labyrinth*, 114, 116; *In Evil Hour*, 110–112; *The Incredible and Sad Tale of Innocent Erendira and Her Heartless Grandmother*, 114; *Leafstorm*, 99, 106, 108–109; *Love in the Times of Cholera*, 114, 116; *No One Writes to the Colonel*, 106, 109–113, 116; *Of Love and Other Demons*, 114; *One Hundred Years of Solitude*, xvi, 65-66, 72, 97, 101, 113–114, 116; *Strange Pilgrims*, 114

Gardel, Carlos, 52
Garzón, Luis Eduardo, 124
Gaviria, César, 103
Gaviria, Víctor, 68
Génesis, 76
Geography, 1
Gil, Aníbal, 120
Gil, Heriberto, 53
Giraldo Castro, Alberto, 66
Gómez, Laureano, 17, 54
Gómez, Pedro Nel, 118, 123, 127
Gómez Agudelo, Fernando, 44
Gómez Jaramillo, Ignacio, 118
Góngora, Leonel, 120
González, Beatriz, 118, 121
González Camargo, Joaquín, 86
Grau, Enrique, 117–120
Greater Antioquia: history and features, 2–4; traditional dress, 28; traditional music, 73. *See also* Literature
Greater Cauca: history and features, 5–6; traditional dance, 33; traditional music, 73. *See also* Literature
Greiff, León de, 85
Grillo, Max, 70
Groot, José Manuel, 85
"Group of Barranquilla," 37, 66, 82, 99, 102, 118
Grupo Niche, 77
Guerrero, Alfredo, 122
Gutiérrez, Alfredo, 74
Gutiérrez González, Gregorio, 84

Henao Gaviria, Antonio, 52–53
History: Constitution of 1863, 10; Constitution of 1886, 10, 16; early twentieth century, 11; formative years, 10; independence, 10; Regeneration, 10–11; *La Revolución en Marcha*, 11; Spanish conquest, 9. *See also* La Violencia
Hosie, Eduardo, 124

Industries, 12

Inravisión (Instituto Nacional de Radio y Televisión), 44–47
Interior highland: history and features, 2; traditional dance, 31–32; traditional dress, 27–28; traditional music, 73. *See also* Literature
Isaacs, Jorge, 90–91

Jaramillo, Oscar, 122
Jaramillo, Roberto, 50
Jaramillo Agudelo, Darío, 95
Judaism, 22

Lagarto, 39–40
Lara, Fernando Charry, 86
Lara, Rodrigo, 48
Lemaitre, Daniel, 74
Lemus López, Marino, 71
León Giraldo, Diego, 66
Literature: Caribbean Coast, 82–84; greater Antioquia, 84–85; greater Cauca, 90–92; greater Tolima, 88–90; historical background, 81–82; interior highland, 85–88; modern literature, 92–96. *See also under specific names of authors*
Llanos, Antonio, 90
Lleras Camargo, 53
Loochkartt, Angel, 120
López, Luis Carlos, 82
López Michelsen, Alfonso, 79, 92, 103
López Pumarejo, Alfonso, 11, 51–52, 126
Lozano, Margarita, 121

M-19, urban guerrilla movement, 12
"Manoello," 75
Mantilla Caballero, Jorge, 120
Marroquín, José Manuel, 10, 85, 87
Marroquín, Lorenzo, 70, 87
Martínez, Carlos, 127, 129
Martínez Rivas, 70
Martínez Silva, Carlos, 60
Marulanda, Octavio, 71
Maya, Rafael, 90

Mayolo, Carlos, 67
Media. *See* Press; Radio; Television
Meira, Mónica, 121
Mejía Vallejo, Manuel, 80, 85
Mesa, Yolanda, 124
Mesa Nicholls, Salvador, 71
Mestre, Goar (and brother Abel), 44
Mito, 85–87, 92
Morales, Darío, 122–123
Moreno-Durán, R. H., 80, 95–96
El mosaico, 82, 85, 88, 91
Mújica, Elisa, 37
Mundial de Fútbol, 26–27
Muñoz, Oscar, 122
Music, 63–64, 72–78; *bolero*, 74–76; *cumbia*, 74; regional music, 73; rock, 76; *salsa*, 72, 76–78; *vallenato*, 73
Mutis, Alvaro, 86, 94–95

Nadaísmo (and the *nadaístas*), 63, 71, 93
Nariño Alvarez, Antonio Amador José, 58–59
Negreiros, María Teresa, 122
Negret, Edgar, 117–118, 120, 123
Newspapers. *See* Press
Nieto, Juan José, 82–83
Norden, Francisco, 66–67
Los Nuevos, 85–86, 90
Núñez, Rafael, 7, 10

Obeso, Candelario, 70, 82
Obregón, Alejandro, 66, 82, 99, 117–119, 123
Obregón, Carlos, 86
Ochoa, Calixto, 74
ODIPE (Oficina de Información y Prensa del Estado), 44
Ojo al cine (magazine of film critique), 68
Olaya Herrera, Enrique, 11, 50, 126
Orozco Morales, Efraín, 75
Ortiz, José, 60
Osorio, Luis Enrique, 70
Osorio Lizarazo, José Antonio, 9, 87–88

Ospina, Hernando de, 69
Ospina, Luis, 67
Ospina, Pedro Nel, 49
Oviedo, Héctor F., 124

Painting, 118–124; Bachué movement, 118; classical style, 121; experimental works, 122; expressionism, 121; political themes, 122; "pop" painter, 121–122; realism, 122; surrealism, 121; universal movement, 118. *See also under specific names of principal artists*
Palacios, Arnold, 90
Palanca, 39
Palenques, 4
Pambalé, "Kid," 36
Pardo, Jorge Eliécer, 89, 94
Pardo García, Germán, 86
Paredes, Demetrio, 124
Parra Sandoval, Rodrigo, 95
Pastrana, Misael, 19
Pellet Buitrago, Elías, 50
Peña, Luis David, 65
Pérez, Juana, 124
Photography, 124–125
Piedra y Cielo, 86, 90
Pinto, Jorge, 66
Plastic arts, 117–124; sculpture, 123–124. *See also* Painting
Pombo, Rafael, 86
Potdevin, Philip, 96
Press (newpapers), 43, 56–62; early newspapers, 57–58; journalism's beginnings, 58–59; nineteenth century, 59–60; printing press in Latin America, 57; the Regeneration and, 60; twentieth century, 61–62
Protestant Church, 22
Pulido, Jorge Enrique, 48

Racines, Julio, 124
Radio, 43, 49–56; *Bogotazo* and government control, 53–54; contemporary period, 55–56; cultural and educational radio, 54–55; inception, 49–51; radio journalism, 52–53; rapid growth and commercialization, 51–53
Ramírez, Eduardo, 118
Ramírez, José Tomás, 64, 69
Ramírez Gaviria, Enrique, 50–51
Ramírez Villamizar, Eduardo, 118–120, 123
Rayo, Omar, 117, 120
RCN (Radio Cadena Nacional), 55–56
Regionalism: causes, 6–7; historical development and causes, 7–8; introduction, 2; national unification, 8–9. *See also under names of specific regions*
Reinado de Belleza, 26–27, 29
Rengifo, Luis Angel, 122
Rentería, Edgar, 37
Restrepo Suárez, Fernando, 46
Reyes, Carlos José, 72
Rivas Groot, José Manuel, 70, 87
Rivera, José Eustacio, 88–89
Roda, Juan Antonio, 120
Rodas Isaza, Gustavo, 52
Rodríguez, Marta, 67, 122
Rodríguez, Melitón, 124–125
Rodríguez Freyle, Juan, 79
Rojas, Carlos, 123
Rojas, Jorge, 86
Rojas, Miguel Angel, 122
Rojas Herazo, Héctor, 93–94
Rojas Pinilla, Gustavo, 44–45, 54, 61, 85
Román, Celso, 124
Roman Catholic Church, 15; Catholic Social Action (Catholic Action), 18–19; celebrations, 26, 29; Concordat of 1887 and, 16; Constitution of 1886 and, 16; education, 16; evangelization, 16; missionaries, 16; new concordat of the 1970s, 19; other institutional religions, 22–23; Popes John XXIII and Paul VI, 20; religious and social practices today, 20–22; La Violencia and, 17
Romero de Nohra, Rocío, 95

Ruiz, Jorge Eliécer, 86

Salcedo, Monsignor José Joaquín, 18, 35
Salgado Mejía, Fabio ("Estéfano"), 63, 76
Samper, Daniel, 61
Samper, Darío, 86
Samper, Ernesto, 41
Samper, José María, 60, 80, 88
Sánchez, Héctor, 89, 94
Sánchez Juliao, David, 48, 80, 94
Santander, Kike, 76
Santos, Eduardo, 60
Schroeder, Carlos E., 65
Sculpture, 123–124
Segundo Silvestre, Luis, 85
Senn, Martha, 63
Silva, Jorge, 67
Silva, José Asunción, 86
Soto Borda, Clímaco, 87
Sports, 35–37; baseball, 36–37; bicycling, 36; boxing, 36; bullfighting, 36; *fútbol* (soccer), 35–36
Suárez, Marco Fidel, 11, 86
Syncretism, 21

Tadeo Lozano, Jorge, 58
TEC (Teatro Experimental de Cali), 71–71
Tejada, Lucy, 121
Television, 43–49; commercialization, 45; education, 48; expansion, 46; inception, 44–45; in Latin America, 44; in politics, 45–46; programming contentions, 47; *telenovelas*, 47–48
Televisora Nacional, 44–46
Téllez, Hernando, 50–51
Theater, 63–64, 69–72; colonial period, 69; contemporary theater, 71–72; early twentieth century, 70–71; eighteenth and nineteenth centuries, 69–70; oral tradition and, 69
TODELAR (Tobón de la Roche), 55–56
Torres, Father Camilo, 17–19, 66–67

Turbay, Paula, 37

Urban social customs, 38–40
Uribe, Pedro Antonio, 91–92
Uribe de Estrada, María Helena, 95
Uribe Uribe, Rafael, 125
UTC (Unión de Trabajadores de Colombia), 18

Valencia, Gerardo, 90
Valencia, Guillermo, 90
Valencia Goelkel, Hernando, 86
Vallejo, Fernando, 94
Vanegas, Tiberio, 122
Varela, Eduardo, 86
Varela, Mariana, 122
Vargas, Germán, 66, 82, 99
Vargas Osorio, Tomás, 86
Vargas Tejada, Luis, 69–70
Vargas Vila, José María, 87
Vayda, Ronny, 124
Velásquez, Rodolfo, 121
Vélez de Piedrahita, Rocío, 94
Vergara, Sofía, 37
Vergara y Vergara, José María, 70, 82
Villar, José Dionisio de, 64
Villar, Nicolasa, 64
Vinyes, Ramón, 82
La Violencia, 12; in film, 67; in literature, 89, 92–93, 98, 111–112; in painting, 122; population shifts, 128; press and, 61; radio and, 53–54; Roman Catholic Church and, 17
Viteri, Alicia, 121
Vives, Carlos, 63
Voces, 82, 83

Women's roles, 37–38

Zalamea Borda, Eduardo, 87
Zalamea Borda, Jorge, 54
Zapata Olivella, Manuel, 93
Zea Hernández, Alvaro, 71
Zuluaga, Luz Marina, 37

About the Authors

RAYMOND LESLIE WILLIAMS is Professor of Latin American Literature and Chair of the Department of Hispanic Studies at the University of California, Riverside. He was the founding president of the Association of North American Colombianists (1984–1985). He has published numerous articles and written several books on Latin American literature, two recent ones being *The Modern Latin American Novel* (1998) and *The Writings of Carlos Fuentes* (1996).

KEVIN G. GUERRIERI is completing his Ph.D. at the University of California, Riverside, on the twentieth-century Latin American narrative.

Recent Titles in
Culture and Customs of Latin America and the Caribbean

Culture and Customs of Argentina
David William Foster, Melissa Fitch Lockhart, and Darrell B. Lockhart